TEN TORTURED WORDS

TEN TORTURED WORDS

How the Founding Fathers Tried to
Protect Religion in America . . .
and What's Happened Since

Stephen Mansfield

Thomas Nelson
Since 1798

NASHVILLE   DALLAS   MEXICO CITY   RIO DE JANEIRO   BEIJING

Published in Nashville, TN, by Thomas Nelson. Thomas Nelson is a trademark of Thomas Nelson, Inc.

Thomas Nelson, Inc., titles may be purchased in bulk for educational, business, fund-raising, or sales promotional use. For information, please e-mail SpecialMarkets@ThomasNelson.com.

Library of Congress Cataloging-in-Publication Data
Mansfield, Stephen, 1958-
    Ten tortured words : how the founding fathers tried to protect religion in America . . . and what's happened since / by Stephen Mansfield.
        p. cm.
    Includes bibliographical references and index.
    ISBN 10: 1-59555-084-4
    ISBN 13: 1-59555-084-2
    1. Church and state—United States—History. 2. Freedom of religion—United States. 3. United States. Constitution. 1st Amendment.
I. Title.
KF4865.M29 2007
342.7308'52—dc22

                                                          2007013017
Printed in the United States of America
07 08 09 10 QWM 1 2 3 4 5 6

To my children,
Jonathan and Elizabeth,
and the faithful in their generation

"That which thy fathers bequeathed thee,
Earn it anew if thou would'st possess it."

—*A Celtic Maxim*

CONTENTS

INTRODUCTION

The words alone are uninspiring. They are, like the document in which we find them, more procedure than poetry, more policy than prose. None of the grand language of the American drama is here. There is nothing to rival Thomas Jefferson's "when in the course of human events" or Abraham Lincoln's "new nation conceived in liberty."

Instead, the words are prohibitive, almost angry. They explain what must not be done by an institution that had done it for far too many centuries and to the detriment of the human soul. Throughout most of history, the priest and the king had been one. Thus, from the days of ancient Babylon to the imperial spread of Rome, from the god-kings of Asia to the royal "Defenders of the Faith" in Europe, religious obedience had been commanded by the State. Dissenters were banished or tortured or killed.

But no more. In this American *Novus Ordo Seclorum*, in this "new order of the ages," religion would thrive, but the State would not command it. The wisdom of faith would always be welcomed into the corridors of political power, but the dictates of faith would always be left to the individual conscience and the liberated mind.

So when the fathers of America had fashioned their covenant, their Constitution, and sought—in truth, as an afterthought—to secure the rights of the individual against the strength of government, they told the most powerful institution in their new nation what it must not do:

"Congress shall make no law respecting an establishment of religion."

These were the first ten words of the American Bill of Rights, and they were a miracle of history. For the first time in human experience, the legislative power of a nation was forbidden from legislating the conscience of man. There would be no establishment of religion, no state church or official religion. Faith would be celebrated but not commanded. Worship would be protected but not prescribed. The fathers had even guaranteed it with a second phrase they added to these historic first ten words. Not only would Congress "make no law respecting an establishment of religion," but it would also never "prohibit the free exercise thereof." Together the sixteen words stood guard on the ramparts of the new nation against the tyrannical tendencies of the centuries.

And religion thrived. The institutions of faith multiplied, religious revivals transformed whole communities, and immigrant faiths were welcomed, though not always without initial challenge. The elected representatives of the people, recognizing that religion was essential to the brand of national character that allowed free institutions to flourish, fanned the flames of faith. The people's Congress ordered the printing of Bibles, called for days of prayer and fasting, positioned chaplains in the armed services as well as in its own assemblies, funded missionaries to the natives of the land, and even sponsored church services in government buildings, as we shall see. It was not paradise, but it was an attempt on the part of a national government to encourage religion in general without demanding religion in particular.

Meanwhile, the individual states that had created this federal government were permitted to be as religious as they wanted to be. They were, after all, close to the people. They were local and ethnic and near. Their constitutions could honor whatever faith the people held dear, and their schools could require competence in whatever truths the people wished to pass on to the next generation. It was the *national* Congress that had been addressed in the ten historic words because everyone understood that this *national* Congress had to be bound tight against the expansive arrogance of political power: *"Congress shall make no law respecting an establishment of religion."* States could do as they pleased because their citizens could always vote a change or move elsewhere in the country. There was no escaping the reach of the national Congress, though.

So it was in America, and not just at the dawn of the nation's life. For 150 years, this delicate religious balance prevailed. There would be no national church, but there would be national encouragement of faith. There would be no official religion, but the states could nurture as vibrant a faith as the people wished. So solid was this arrangement, so clear this vision of religion and government, that the Supreme Court was not even called upon to issue a ruling directly related to it until just after World War II, more than a century and a half after the defining words were first penned.

Yet that ruling was a disaster. In 1947, the majority opinion in a case called *Everson v. Board of Education* dismantled the wise configuration of the American fathers and erected instead a confusing and nearly unenforceable mishmash of prohibitions. The Supreme Court forbade the federal government from passing laws that aid religion or using tax money "in any amount" to support religion or religious institutions.[1] It was a break from history, a break from the plain sense of the ten noble words, and, for reasons to be discussed later in these pages, it was a prohibition that applied not only to the federal government but to the states as well.

To justify this rejection of the American fathers' design, the Supreme Court cited the words of a letter written by Thomas Jefferson and concluded that the intent of the first ten words of the First Amendment was to erect "a wall of separation between church and state." It did not matter that Thomas Jefferson wrote this letter some fourteen years after the First Amendment became law. It did not matter that Thomas Jefferson was not even in the country during the convention that drafted the First Amendment. Nor did it matter that Jefferson's words were used in a manner that Jefferson himself would not have approved. What *did* seem to matter was a new and secular vision for the nation, one that was far removed from anything the founding generation had envisioned.

The dismantling of a heritage thus began. With the Supreme Court forbidding government to touch religion in any way, an entire industry of litigation was born. During the following decades there were lawsuits to chisel religious phrases from official buildings, strip the Ten Commandments from schools and government buildings, quash prayer in any form at any governmentally connected event, end religious instruction in public schools, banish religious symbols from state or federal land, remove chaplains from legislatures and the armed services, and even to keep religion from playing a role in the rehabilitation of criminals.

It grew worse. In the secularist climate of the *Everson* aftermath, a young senator from Texas decided that he had endured enough political opposition from religious organizations. These faith-based groups persisted in exposing his corruption and in pointing out abuses in the election that had landed him in office. So in 1954, Senator Lyndon Johnson proposed an amendment to the tax code that would silence the political speech of religious, tax-exempt organizations. Now, not only was government kept from supporting religion, but religion was kept from speaking its wisdom into the processes of government.

To preserve this secular vision, new organizations arose, such as People for the American Way, the Freedom from Religion Foundation, and Americans United for the Separation of Church and State. Even the American Civil Liberties Union, from time to time a valiant defender of traditional liberties, turned its energies toward

banning the vestiges of traditional religion in   a cr
And the efforts of these organizations were rich   lan
largely through the perversion of an otherwise b   of t

In 1976, the courts began ruling that victims o   Mu
could have their legal fees paid if they were victor   fev
reclaim what had been taken from them. These rulin   fie
for example, to encourage a black man in Alabama to
employment discrimination without fear of losing hi   m
the process. It was a noble pillar in the temple of Ameri
but in time the courts began applying this law to relig   b
allowing third parties to benefit. This meant that the AC   i
a lawsuit to have a cross removed from a state park, an
could not only force the state to remove the cross but als
pay the ACLU's legal fees. With incentives such as these, s
America became a profit-making venture.

Intimidation quickly became the tactic of choice. A sc
trict might permit a Bible study to meet on school proper
class hours. This would offend the ACLU, which would in tu
tact the district and threaten a lawsuit. It would only re
threat. The financially strapped school district knew it did n
the resources for a protracted legal war. Moreover, the ACLU
make sure that the school district understood that a loss in
would mean paying both its own and the ACLU's legal expense
was too great a risk. The school district would ban the Bible st
without putting up a fight, and the ACLU would emerge victorio
through sheer intimidation. It was faith-based blackmail at its be
It was also the state-funded dismantling of a centuries-old heritag
of faith.

This, then, is the post-*Everson* world we live in today. In the present climate, a single atheist files a suit to remove the name of God
from the pledge of allegiance, a court hears arguments as to whether

ss on the Los Angeles County seal is a violation of the law of the
, military chaplains are sometimes forbidden to pray in the name
he very God whom they have sworn to serve in arms, and when
slims in a Florida school district ask to be released from classes a
days a year to practice their faith, that school district is so terri-
d it bans all religious holidays in fear of legal bombardment.

All of this is based on ten now tortured words: "Congress shall
ake no law respecting an establishment of religion."

As the average American looks on, he is hardly surprised. He has
een schooled to believe that the law is a plaything among lawyers. This
s what the O. J. Simpson debacle, political scandals in Washington DC,
and the courtroom antics of celebrity trials have taught him. He laughs
with pained understanding at the latest lawyer joke and is knowingly
amused when a commentator on television quotes the centuries-old
line from Shakespeare's *King Henry VI*: "The first thing we do, let's kill
all the lawyers."[2]

That American might have felt differently. He remembers the pride
he felt those years ago in elementary school when he quoted the preamble to the Constitution for the school play. He sensed that the words
were holy, not in a divine sense, but in the way that a people make
something holy by their reverence. Later, in high school, he wrote a
paper on the Electoral College and marveled at the wisdom of those
founding minds two centuries before. But that has faded. Though, if he
is average among his countrymen, he believes in God, prays regularly,
and wants his leaders to be moral—even righteous—people, he does
not expect the Constitution that rules his land to preserve anything of
a noble heritage. Law is what the judges say it is, he believes. If statistics
are true, he is more likely to know the names of all the cartoon characters in the hit television show *The Simpsons* than he is to know the five
rights guaranteed to him in the First Amendment.[3]

Here, then, is where our average American might have lived out his

days: in the litigious, cynical vacuum of a vanishing public religion. But then something remarkable happened: religion once again moved center stage in American culture. It is difficult to say exactly when this began. Perhaps it was the transforming experience of September 11, 2001. Perhaps it was the spiritual hunger of the Baby Boomers and their children, the Millennials—together nearly two hundred million strong—that dragged the nation in tow toward a reconsideration of spirituality. Or perhaps it was the religious re-examination forced by the American experience at war and the reality that the nation's greatest enemy in the world was a religious network violently making a moral/spiritual case against the West and against the United States in particular.

Whatever the cause, this religious awakening has become one of the most defining hallmarks of recent American history, and it is forcing a reconsideration of the role of religion in American national life and thus of the meaning of those ten tortured words: "Congress shall make no law respecting an establishment of religion." Was this single sentence really designed to banish faith from the American public square? Did the founding generation really intend a secular State, or did they intend a religious society encouraged but unhindered by the State? Has the *Everson* legacy robbed the nation of the religious wisdom of the founding fathers at a time when she is in desperate need of it, at a time when faith is reclaiming a defining role at the center of American culture?

The present American moment—when a religiously inspired global war, a religiously inspired president, an increasingly religious population, and religiously inflamed politics all shape the national experience—seems a perfect moment for the reconsideration of our religious heritage and of the laws that have banished the wisdom of that heritage from our public life. The truth is that the sixty-year legacy of the Supreme Court's *Everson* decision has tortured the intent of the founding generation, tortured the vital role of religion in a civil society, and tortured the emergent faith that now offers an American renaissance. Perhaps this present American moment gives us opportunity to grant the next generation a greater legacy than we have received.

1

WHAT THE
FATHERS FOUNDED

The revolution is well underway. And the people rejoice. "Liberty" is the cry heard on the streets, and with every blow against the king, with every stab at the old order, the electric sense of a new age dawning fills the already charged air.

Now it is time for the real enemy to fall: religion. It is religion, after all, that dulls the minds of the people and religion that justifies the corruptions of monarchs and churchmen. Now, finally, the tyranny of faith over the minds of men will be brought to an end.

Already steps have been taken. The Christian calendar has been replaced by a new one in honor of the revolution. Now, instead of a seven-day week with a Sabbath, there will be a ten-day week with a day of rest. Churches have been declared State property, clergymen have been forced to swear allegiance to the nation, and laws based on Christian ethics have been revised.

Today, though, the grand transformation will occur. Today, a new faith fit for a new nation will arise.

In the greatest church in the land, which sits proudly at the heart of the capital city, the president and the secretaries, the people's representatives and the generals, have already gathered. They, like the thickening crowd, are nervous with anticipation. Fortunately, they are not made to wait long. The ceremony begins, signaled by the eruption of dancing. It is ecstatic, convulsive. Throughout the pillared sanctuary, bands of dancers gyrate, their movements accented by their near nakedness. Bare-breasted with only the slightest clothing at the waists and their stockings gathered at their feet, these nymph-like beings leap and swirl, the flash of a sweat-glistened breast

3

visible here, the arch of a well-muscled buttock rising there. It is erotic and thrilling to the crowd. Some, able to withstand it no longer, quickly steer an unsuspecting partner to a dark corner of the church to answer their rising lust.

Then, the soar of trumpets, and all eyes turn up the center aisle of the church to the ornate entrance at the rear. It is the grand procession. The dancing grows more frenzied and into view comes a woman seated upon a chair that is borne aloft by poles on the shoulders of a dozen men. The woman wears a red cap and is framed by a bright blue cape. She is heavily rouged and nearly naked, and as she seems to float above the heads of her attendants, the crowd begins kissing the air in her direction. It is their due act of worship, for this woman is the Goddess of Reason.

The adoration rises to shouts of ecstasy, the explosion of voices deafening in the great, stony expanse of the church as the procession continues to the front of the crowd and slows. The goddess's chair is moved by her bearers from their shoulders to the large, high table that is the object of every seat in the church. This was once the high altar of a Christian church. It is now the throne of the Goddess of Reason, and as she takes her place the assembly erupts into full-throated singing of the "Hymn to Liberty." There are tears as hands are raised aloft in honor of the moment.

With the "Hymn" completed, the joyous celebration begins. Hypnotic pulsations of music explode at full volume, and there is mad, heated dancing both within the church and around the bonfires outside. The crowd surrounding the building grows, pulsates, thrills. A form of liturgy is observed within. Canoneers, with pipes of tobacco jutting from their mouths, serve at the altar of the goddess. Wheelbarrows of objects formerly used in Christian worship—censers, communion plates, crosses, and chandeliers—are offered to the goddess, her reward for victory over all previous gods.

Liquor is soon introduced into the celebration, and even children stumble about under its influence, much to the raucous amusement of the crowd. Young girls don the vestments formerly used by Christian priests and dance about the room, taking the hands of men who were once clergymen but who now are nearly entranced in the worship of the goddess. Some—believing that the more the Christian God is renounced, the more the Goddess of Reason reigns—shout obscenities to the Christian God and curse Him as a fraud.

As the day drifts into the dim light of evening, the revelry spreads throughout the city, the gathering dark of night broken by fires splashing light on ecstatic, dancing throngs. There is much to celebrate. All men know the truth now. The Revolution is complete. The secular State is born. Reason reigns and religion is dead. Long live the Revolution![1]

IT WAS KARL MARX WHO SAID THAT "A PEOPLE WITHOUT A HERITAGE are easily persuaded." He might also have said that a heritage forgotten or misremembered has the same effect, and in few countries on earth is this more starkly illustrated than in the United States.

Under the press of world events and a nagging sense of internal aimlessness, America today is struggling to define who she is. Not surprisingly, this struggle often takes the form of a war of remembrance, a contest of competing visions of history. The combatants understand that while the past is indeed prologue, as Shakespeare wrote, it is also prophecy. The nation will ultimately be defined by what she remembers herself to have been—whether that memory is factual or not. Nowhere is this proving truer than in the national memory of religion.

In the vignette that opens this chapter, a secular State arises, purposefully casting off the shackles of traditional religion. Faith is outlawed, churches are confiscated, and clergymen are made to renounce their vows. Society is cleansed of all religious influence, and the foundation is laid for a legal system that will jealously guard the people against the encroachment of all gods.

This is how the American Revolution is often remembered. In fact, it is not going too far to say that for those who seek a secular America today, this *is* the founding vision. The United States, they believe, was intended at least in part as a rejection of European Christianity. Accordingly, the founding documents were carefully crafted to assure that the tyrannies of faith would never do to the new nation what they had done to the beleaguered kingdoms of the Old World. That the First Amendment should erect an impenetrable wall of separation between the sacred and the secular, assuring that the former should never trouble the latter, is exactly what the founding fathers hoped.

Yet the scene that opens this chapter is not taken from the American Revolution. Nor did anything of its kind ever occur during the American Revolution. It is, instead, an episode from the French Revolution. It was the French Revolution that angrily rejected Christianity, that enthroned a Goddess of Reason on the high altar at Notre Dame, and that sought to eradicate every vestige of Christian influence upon the law, the government, and the culture as a whole. Indeed, it was in the French Revolution that the secular State was born.

Nothing of the kind would have crossed the minds of the majority of the American founding fathers, though. By November of 1793, when Notre Dame was renamed the "Temple of Reason" and an actress was enthroned as a goddess upon her altar/throne, the Americans had already issued their Declaration of Independence to the world, fought their revolution, and crafted their Constitution with its Bill of Rights.[2] Indeed, as news of the revolution in France reached the American founders, most were repulsed.[3] Writing to his friend, the Marquis de Lafayette—who was embroiled in the events of the French Revolution at the time—Alexander Hamilton captured the horror of his generation of Americans:

> When I contemplate the horrid and systematic massacres of the Jacobins . . . when I find the doctrines of Atheism openly advanced in the convention and heard with loud applause . . . I acknowledge that I am glad to believe there is no real resemblance between what was the cause of America and what is the cause of France; that the difference is no less great than the difference between liberty and licentiousness.[4]

Of course, not everyone of Hamilton's generation felt as he did. Founding fathers like Thomas Paine and Ethan Allen would later embrace the French values and may have looked back upon the reign of Notre Dame's Goddess of Reason with longing. Still, the majority of the American founders viewed the French experience as the very sort of excess that they sought to guard against in their own revolution.

Despite such protests, the American Revolution is often misremembered as the French Revolution. From the classroom to the courtroom, this widespread fiction lives on, transforming the American Revolution into the antireligion upheaval of a secularist's dream. One of the most absurd expressions of this distortion came in the 1985 movie *Revolution*. Though it starred the brilliant Al Pacino and was directed by Hugh Hudson, fresh from an Oscar win for *Chariots of Fire*, the film almost ruined the careers of both men. Perhaps part of the reason for this was its peculiar portrayal of the American Revolution in French terms. Characters went about addressing each other as "Citizen" and sporting the red caps of the Jacobins—who came to power in France nearly a decade after the events depicted in the film! Property was confiscated and sons of colonists were conscripted at gunpoint. Clergymen were treated with disdain, and the script goes to great pains to portray the decline of religion among the people. Clearly, this is the French experience transplanted to American soil with dramatic license, but it is not history.

One suspects that such fabrications are the result neither of accident nor of ignorance. One suspects, instead, that the French revolutionary experience is often overlaid upon the American experience because some wish it were so, because such revisionism is essential to creating a secular America. As the dean of American conservatism, William Buckley Jr., has said, "What we are up against, in both the academy and the judiciary, is a felt disappointment that the American Revolution was not the French Revolution, and a consequent attempt to Jacobinize the Constitution until religion and its influence are wholly banished from our public life."[5]

The truth is that the American colonial experience, the American Revolution, and the American founding documents were so shaped by traditional religion, and intended as extensions of traditional religion, as to be an embarrassment to the advocates of a secular American State. Thus the revisionism. Thus the borrowing of the French legacy. Thus the fabricated national memory that not only seeks to distort the official history of the nation but which has also fueled a radical and destructive misreading of the first ten words of the American Bill of Rights.

This said, it is not hard to understand why most Americans today have difficulty appreciating the depth and grandeur of the religious passion that shaped the world of our founding fathers. We live in an age that partitions and privatizes religion, that is suspicious of zeal and hardened by the cynical religious gush employed by public figures to cover a multitude of sins. We are an age hungry for God yet suspicious of how He is invoked by our neighbors. When we listen to the religious language of our founders, then, we find ourselves tempted to doubt them. It is hard for us to trust that they believed what they wrote and that their great adventures were the offerings to God they said they were.

Yet consider this: In 1620, some one hundred Pilgrims, one-third of them children, boarded a ship no larger than a volleyball court and sailed it for sixty-six days across the North Atlantic. They had departed late in the year, so they arrived in the howling wilderness of New England during winter time and were only kept alive by the help of some friendly Indians and their few remaining supplies from the ship. Still, half of them died during a starving time so severe that not one family was untouched by the loss of a loved one. They passed the first winter, changed their farming methods in the spring, and brought in a good harvest in the fall of 1621. And they survived. We remember them every Thanksgiving and are ennobled by their story.

Naturally, our age wants to know: Why did they do it? Was it to escape religious persecution? No, they weren't being persecuted in Holland where they had lived the twelve years before they sailed. Was it for riches? No, there is no mention of this as a motive in their journals, and they had no reason to expect that wealth might come to them in the New World when they considered the stories of the earlier settlements like Roanoke and Jamestown.

Why did they do it, then? Well, they told us, but we have difficulty believing it. It is rarely mentioned in the textbooks and is scoffed at in the more scholarly publications. Yet before these Pilgrims disembarked their ship, the *Mayflower*, they signed a compact in which they said they sailed "for the glory of God and the advancement of the Christian faith."[6] Given the evidence, it seems that it really was just that simple: a band of a hundred Christians from a congregation in exile decided to try to carry the gospel of Jesus Christ to the New World. So they did the unimaginable: they crossed a stormy, freezing ocean for the glory of God. Our age longs to grasp such heroism, but we find ourselves skeptical and searching for some other, more accessible story.

9

The same is true of the famous voyage to the New World spearheaded by John Winthrop. Leading a flotilla of five ships filled with Puritans across the Atlantic to build a "Bible Commonwealth," Winthrop ordered the ships tied up together a few days off the shore of England and then preached the most defining sermon in American history. His words framed what has come to be known as the "American Covenant."

> Thus stands the cause between God and us: we are entered into covenant with him for this work; we have taken out a commission; the Lord hath given us leave to draw our own articles . . . Now if the Lord shall please to hear us, and bring us in peace to the place we desire, then hath he ratified this covenant and sealed our commission.
>
> For we must consider that we shall be as a city upon a hill. The eyes of all people are upon us. So that if we shall deal falsely with our God in this work we have undertaken, and so cause him to withdraw his present help from us, we shall be made a story and a byword throughout the world.[7]

Modern Americans read these words and are hard pressed to believe that their forefathers seriously thought they had made a covenant with God for the new nation. Even more difficult to accept is that the words and the covenant lived on, renewed in the faith of passing generations of Americans. Indeed, when Ronald Reagan spoke with misty eyes about an American city upon a hill, he was out of step with his generation, and so he was roundly criticized, but he was very much in step with the faith of the founding generations.

What we quickly come to understand is that when we delve into the founding era of America, we are visiting a foreign country of faith that is far removed from our own. The modern American views his faith as a private matter that makes no claims upon his neighbor. For those who settled the English colonies of America, though, faith was not merely a matter of the heart to be lived out in seclusion without disturbing anyone. For them, faith was a commitment to God that came with a blueprint for changing the world, and it is this very matter of the muscular reach of colonial faith that helps us to understand what was intended by the first ten words to the American Bill of Rights.

We must remember that when the *Mayflower* sailed in 1620, it had only been 103 years since Luther posted his Ninety-five Theses on the door of the Wittenberg Castle and 56 years since the death of John Calvin. The titanic matters of faith in question during the lifetimes of these giants were far more than matters of the heart alone; they were matters of the truths by which men might live in the world. What Calvin and Luther engineered transformed men's understanding of government and law, church and education, even language and art. They battled for worldviews that had implications for every area of life.

The early settlers of America were their spiritual children and carried with them to the New World the same sense that the Bibles under their arms were blueprints for the society they hoped to build. Nowhere was this more evident than in their thinking about government. Calvin had taught that while the church and the state were separate institutions, it was not true that one was religious and the other was secular. Instead, Calvin taught that both church and state were instituted by God and were accountable to biblical truth. In other words, they were separate in function, but alike in faith. Both were religious entities; both were ministries. The church was a ministry of the grace and truth of God, the state a ministry of the justice of God.

The society this theology of government created is a far cry from anything we expect faith to build today. For many years in colonial New England, a man involved in a lawsuit could plead his own case in court using the family Bible. Because the work of the state was as biblically based as the work of the church, each principle of law, each policy of government was carefully derived from Scripture. Indeed, in the early 1800s, a law student who had never been very religious found that he had to buy a Bible to fully understand the laws discussed in his textbooks. This was because each principle of law he encountered was attended by a long list of Scripture references, and the young law student was forced to look up each verse to understand what was being taught. In time, the student digested so much Scripture that he underwent a religious conversion. This student's name was Charles Finney, and he became the Billy Graham of his day, yet his story of faith is testament to the broad and beefy brand of religion that was laid at the foundation of this country.

This essential difference between how we view religion today and how it was viewed in the decades from the first settlements through the American Revolution has more to do with its scope than its depth. Men may believe no less ardently today, but they do not expect what they believe to govern their actions in every area of life. We are used to compartmentalizing faith, as a man does when he announces that because of his religion he is personally opposed to abortion or personally opposed to the war but that he will vote the exact opposite if given a chance. The religious worldview of the American founding fathers would have had no room and less patience for such thinking. Truth was truth, and it was true for every area of life.

By the time this thinking flowed down to the Revolutionary generation, it had been filtered by experience, but it was no less influential. Our founders believed that good government meant reliance on religion for a variety of reasons. First, the matters of justice, of right and wrong, that government guards are defined by faith. Second, the individual character required of each citizen for a successful society was rooted in faith and in the power of faith to restrain evil. Finally, the object of faith was God, and few living at the time of the American Revolution or the framing of the founding documents would have expected a society to thrive that did not honor God and seek His pleasure.

Though he was writing a century after the creation of the United States, philosopher George Santayana understood the connection between religion and government that shaped the founding genera- tion's worldview. His words are helpful, perhaps particularly because they come from outside the American colonial experience.

> It should be observed that, if a systematic religion is true at all, intru- sion on its part into politics is not only legitimate, but is the very work it comes into the world to do. Being by hypothesis, enlightened super- naturally, it is able to survey the conditions and consequences of any kind of action much better than the wisest legislature . . . so that spheres of systematic religion and politics—far from being independ- ent are in principle identical.[8]

Expressed in different terms, these sentiments sprang readily from the lips and the pens of the American founding fathers. Perhaps the best-known statement of these ideas is found in George Washington's Farewell Address. Written at the end of his public life and in the wake of the French Revolution, Washington's words about religion and citi- zenship were probably meant as a warning against the mood of athe- ism drifting from Europe.

> Of all the dispositions and habits which lead to political prosperity, religion and morality are indispensable supports. In vain would that man claim the tribute of patriotism who should labor to subvert these great pillars of human happiness . . . And let us with caution indulge the supposition that morality can be maintained without religion. Whatever may be conceded to the influence of refined edu- cation on minds of peculiar structure, reason and experience both

forbid us to expect that national morality can prevail in exclusion of religious principle.[9]

This idea that government and even patriotism are impossible without religion is offensive to many today, but it was a pillar of civic thinking in the founding era. One searches in vain to find a man among the founding fathers who did not believe that religion in some form was essential to the success of the State.

This brings us to the framing of the Constitution and to the words that best capture the thinking of the framers about religion. They are a perfect summation of the colonial theology of government and a perfect statement of what the framers of the Constitution intended to accomplish with their work. They come from an often neglected document called the Northwest Ordinance of 1787.

On July 13, 1787, when the Constitutional Convention in Philadelphia was but seven weeks along in its great task, a Massachusetts war hero, medical doctor, and clergyman named Manasseh Cutler asked the Convention to approve a plan for establishing a colony in the Ohio territory. The document issued in answer to this request was a far-reaching ordinance that not only established the process by which Western territories might become states but also forbade slavery in those regions, assured basic liberties, established territorial governments, and even attempted to safeguard the rights of Native Americans. Undoubtedly, the Northwest Ordinance was the most important piece of legislation passed by the Continental Congress apart from the Declaration of Independence.

The Northwest Ordinance included a provision for schools, which proclaimed, "Religion, morality, and knowledge, being necessary to good government and the happiness of mankind, schools and the means of education shall forever be encouraged."[10] It would be difficult to find a sentence more at odds with the contemporary American understanding of government and education or more surprising to most Americans as a statement of the founding fathers' beliefs.

We should consider the ideas contained in these words carefully. First, religion is essential to good government; not tangential to it, not an adornment of it, not a faint memory preceding it. Rather, religion is necessary to it. Moreover, morality is essential to good government, as is knowledge. Perhaps more, religion, morality, and knowledge are essential to human happiness, as well. These things being true, schools should be built. We should remember that most schools at this time were private and religious. This was the era before the rise of public education.

If these words were found only in a colonial sermon or a private letter of the time, they might not be significant. However, they were made law by the very men who drafted the US Constitution. What they confirm is that the idea of a secular State was foreign to the men who assembled during that steamy summer of 1787. The start of the French Revolution, which was the first attempt in history to establish a completely secular political order, was yet two years off, its more radical phase not beginning until five years later in 1792.[11] The men of the Constitutional Convention had not known—nor did they believe it was possible to have—a government that did not rely upon the restraining force of religious morality and that was not an extension of the religious consensus of the people.

How odd, then, that we are asked to believe that these very men drafted a Constitution that banned religion's influence upon government and created a secular State. How odd that their words should be used to drive the influence of religion from the nation's schools. How odd that their document should become the wedge used to dislodge the very vestiges of faith that they themselves would soon set in place.

Clearly, the men who adopted the Northwest Ordinance as law and framed the US Constitution had no intention of driving religion from the public sphere. Yet to understand how their purposes have been perverted, we must first understand the evolution of the first ten words of the Bill of Rights.

Two centuries after the fact, it is odd to realize that the primary reason for opposition to the Bill of Rights among the founding fathers was the belief that they were unnecessary. Some at the time reasoned that since the Constitution had not given the federal government control over guns or religion or the press, for example, there was no reason to worry that the federal government would encroach on these areas. As Alexander Hamilton argued in *The Federalist*, a "Bill of Rights in the sense and to the extent in which they are contended for, are not only unnecessary in the proposed constitution, but would even be dangerous . . . For why declare that things shall not be done which there is no power to do?"[12]

Given the expansive reach of government in our time, we can be thankful for those who expressed an opposite view. Writing from France where he had been during the whole of the Constitutional Convention, Jefferson confided to James Madison, "I will now add what I do not like. First, the omission of the Bill of Rights providing clearly and without the aid of sophisms for freedom of religion, freedom of press, protection against standing armies, restriction against monopolies, the eternal and unremitting force of habeas corpus laws and trials by jury."[13]

Spencer Roane of Virginia held similar views and expressed them in humorous terms: "A Constitution ought to be like Caesar's wife, not only good, but unsuspected, since it is the highest compact which men are capable of forming and involves the dearest rights of life, liberty and property."[14] Thankfully, men of such sentiments prevailed.

It was not without a fight, though, for when the federal government under the new Constitution was declared in effect on March 4, 1789, Rhode Island and North Carolina had yet to ratify the governing document of the land. Madison, who had initially been opposed to the idea of a bill of rights, decided that achieving unity was reason enough for a compromise and determined to lead the way in welcoming the prodigal states "into the bosom of the Confederacy."[15]

It was on that same date, March 4, 1789, that James Madison rose on the floor of the new Congress to announce his intention to introduce amendments to the Constitution. To his disappointment, Congress was not in the same hurry he was. The matter did not come up again until June 8 when Madison finally offered nine formal amendments that were largely suggestions proposed by the various state ratifying committees.

That these early amendments to the Constitution came from the states and not from the floor of Congress makes them critical to understanding the mind of the founding generation. As historian Carl Van Doren has said, "Since among them they protect virtually all the rights which had been urged by the various state conventions, they may be regarded as the contribution of the people through those conventions to the Constitution."[16] Clearly, the people wanted greater protection from the possibility of an overreaching federal government than the Constitution provided, and both the specific protections they urged and the wording of their proposed amendments, particularly in the matter of religion, do much to explain the people's intent in what became the Bill of Rights.

It is certainly true that observing the process of a bill or an amendment working its way through the tedious meat grinders of Congress is as thrilling as watching paint dry. An author asks his readers to follow him through such a journey only at the risk of having his request become the last words read before a deep sleep. In this case, though, the proposals and revisions explain so thoroughly the original purpose of our ten tortured words that the journey is essential and might even be made relatively painless.

Before Madison submitted his nine amendments on June 8, he had already received several suggestions from the states for amendments concerning religious freedom. The amendment he put before Congress was his own reworking of these proposals.

> The civil rights of none shall be abridged on account of religious belief or worship, nor shall any national religion be established, nor shall the full and equal rights of conscience be in any matter, nor on any pretext, infringed.[17]

Two of the phrases in this amendment are no surprise. It is natural in a law to protect religious freedom that both the right of the individual to worship as he wishes and the right to exercise his conscience freely would be mentioned. What is intriguing is the language forbidding a national religion. Obviously, the founding generation had not forgotten its experience with the State Church of England.

Almost any schoolchild who is asked about the cause of the American Revolution will say that the colonists fought against "taxation without representation." Though this is certainly true, it is not the whole story. What is usually not taught in that child's textbooks is the role religion played in prying the colonists from England.

The often neglected truth is that when King George III decided to exact tighter control over the colonies following the costly French and Indian War, he concluded that sending an Anglican bishop to America would serve his purposes. A bishop would enforce Anglicanism—the State religion of England—throughout the colonies, strengthen the authority of the crown, and check the growth of dissenter religions.

He could hardly have designed a plan more likely to incite the colonists against him. A quick survey of the American colonies at the time reveals Congregationalists in the North, Quakers and Catholics in the Middle Colonies, Baptists and Presbyterians everywhere, and

Anglicans with loose control only in the Carolinas and Georgia. None but the southern Anglicans would welcome a bishop with open arms, and most colonists would see the move for what it was: a tentacle of English control destined to strangle colonial liberties.

Heightening the alarm the colonists felt at the news of a bishop on their shores was the stern warning given by the best-known Englishman in the world at the time, the evangelist George Whitefield. Though an Anglican priest himself, Whitefield loved his American cousins and not only preached seven transforming evangelistic crusades from Georgia to Massachusetts but also warned the colonists of the English encroachment upon their liberties. At one meeting, typical of the kind that drew crowds in the tens of thousands, Whitefield closed with these troubling words:

> I can't in conscience leave the town without acquainting you with a secret. My heart bleeds for America. O poor New England! There is a deep laid plot against both your civil and religious liberties, and they will be lost. Your golden days are at an end. You have nothing but trouble before you.[18]

These were more than the rantings of an itinerant preacher. Whitefield was a man revered by the founding generation. Benjamin Franklin loved him and even tried to settle Western territories in partnership with him. Founding fathers like Washington, Adams, and Patrick Henry lauded him. His warnings were heard, and the resolve that grew among the colonists transformed the Revolution into a holy war for many an American.[19]

This is certainly how George III saw the American cause. Though he tried to make light of it, he could not escape the influence of religion among his rebellious American subjects. His attitude was very much that of Prime Minister Horace Walpole, who quipped, "Cousin

America has run off with a Presbyterian parson." As the progress of the war grew more dire for the British, the king confessed that of all the American regiments he most feared "the Black Regiment." By this he did not mean a regiment of African-American soldiers, though blacks fought valiantly in the colonial cause. He meant instead that he feared the regiment of colonial clergymen—remembered by the king in their black preaching robes—who stoked the fires of the American cause by their preaching and ministry.

With religion so much at the heart of the War for Independence, it is not hard to understand why the colonists came to view the king as the anti-Christ and the British forces as minions of darkness. During the Revolutionary War, when British troops captured a colonial church they routinely turned it into a riding stable or a whorehouse. Colonial parsons were summarily killed and colonial Bibles and hymnbooks were burned as outlaw literature. Such horrors were not soon forgotten in the postwar years, and when the framers of the Constitution set about to guard religious liberties in their new nation, they did not hesitate to ban an English-style State Church. No one in Congress was surprised, then, on June 8, 1789, when James Madison's religious liberty amendment forbade a "national religion."

What may also have come as no surprise, given the nature of legislatures, was that Congress referred Madison's amendments to a committee with the pompous name of "Committee of the Whole on the State of the Union," which did nothing for six weeks and thus became obsolete. There was more debate, and finally on July 21 the House of Representatives assigned the matter to a Select Committee, which a week later offered new wording of Madison's original amendment:

> No religion shall be established by law, nor shall the equal rights of conscience be infringed.[20]

The House began debating this proposal on August 15. Congressman Peter Sylvester of New York objected that the language "might be thought to have tendency to abolish religion altogether," something no one wanted to do. Massachusetts's Congressman Eldridge Berry suggested instead the words "no religious doctrine shall be established by law." This didn't hit the mark, there was more debate, and representatives began wrestling for new language.

Samuel Livermore of New Hampshire proposed "Congress shall make no laws touching religion, or infringing the rights of conscience." This pleased some but not all and brought Madison to his feet to defend his original proposal. We should be glad it did and that Madison's words were captured by the House reporter. They allow us to know exactly what Madison understood the purpose of the amendment to be.

> Mr. Madison said, he apprehended the meaning of the words to be, *that Congress should not establish a religion, enforce the legal observation of it by law, nor compel men to worship God in any manner contrary to their conscience.* Whether the words are necessary or not, he did not mean to say, but they had been required by some of the State Conventions, who seemed to entertain an opinion that under the clause of the constitution, which gave power to Congress to make all laws necessary and proper to carry into execution the constitution, and the laws made under it, enabled them to make laws of such a nature as might infringe the rights of conscience, and establish a national religion; to prevent these effects he presumed the amendment was intended, and he thought it as well expressed as the nature of the language would admit.[21] (emphasis added)

This brought some clarity but no return to Madison's draft, and a vote on Livermore's proposal passed 31–20. Five days later, though,

Congressman Fisher Ames of Massachusetts offered a further change that won approval in the House and was sent on to the Senate for consideration:

> Congress shall make no law establishing religion, or to prevent the free exercise thereof, or to infringe the rights of conscience.[22]

Unfortunately, the Senate debates in those days were not recorded, so all we know from the *Senate Journal* is what motions were passed or defeated. We can be sure, then, that the following three versions of the amendment weren't what the Senate had in mind:

> Congress shall make no law establishing one religious sect or society in preference to others, or to infringe on the rights of conscience. *Defeated*
>
> Congress shall not make any law infringing the rights of conscience, or establishing any religious sect or society. *Defeated*
>
> Congress shall make no law establishing any particular denomination of religion in preference to another, or prohibiting the free exercise thereof, nor shall the rights of conscience be infringed. *Defeated*

Finally, on September 9, Oliver Ellsworth of Connecticut proposed an amendment that narrowed the wording considerably:

> Congress shall make no law establishing articles of faith or a mode of worship or prohibiting the free exercise of religion.

This version was approved by the Senate and sent back to the House of Representatives—who weren't impressed. They requested a committee composed of members of the House and the Senate to rework the amendment. This committee, led by Madison, achieved in hours what the House and the Senate had taken weeks to do. By September 24, three days after the joint committee first met, the House approved the committee's new language with the Senate agreeing to it the next day. The first sentence of the First Amendment would read: "Congress shall make no law respecting an establishment of religion, or prohibiting the free exercise thereof."

The language is important. The new law did not simply forbid Congress to erect a State Church or establish an official religion. This goal would have been achieved by most of the proposed amendments we have seen above. Instead, the new law was actually broadened beyond what had been proposed. Congress was not only forbidden to establish an official religion, but it was forbidden to make a law that even dealt with the issue of an establishment of religion. Here we see the states protecting their prerogatives, their authority to establish religion if they chose to. Congress was forbidden to make a law that even touched or treated—this is the meaning of the word *respecting* in context—the matter of an establishment of religion. Therefore, the states' authority to establish religion was protected while Congress's authority to establish religion was cut off. The law was a double-edged sword, but only for Congress and the federal government.

What is clear from the various versions of the amendment and from the snippets of debate included here is this: the purpose of the first ten words of the First Amendment was to forbid a State religion or what Congress called "an establishment of religion." There is no evidence in all the debates and proposed language of an attempt to erect a secular State similar to the one that arose during the French Revolution. There is no evidence of an attempt to keep the government from supporting religion. There is no evidence of any concern that religion might influence government. There was only concern that the government might officially establish a religion that would destroy the religious liberties of the people. That these words, coming as they do from these proceedings, should be construed today as a ban on government support for religion in general is at best ignorance and at worst intellectual dishonesty.

Confirming this is what took place only a few hours after the Congress adopted the First Amendment: Congressman Elias Boudinot of New Jersey proposed that the Congress ask President George Washington to recommend to the American people a day of public thanksgiving and prayer. The very next day, but twenty-four hours after Congress approved the language of the First Amendment, the following resolution was passed:

> Resolved, that a joint committee of both Houses be directed to wait upon the President of the United States, to request that he would recommend to the people of the United States a day of public thanksgiving and prayer, to be observed by acknowledging, with grateful hearts, the many signal favors of Almighty God, especially by affording them an opportunity peaceable to establish a Constitution of government for their safety and happiness.[23]

President Washington was thrilled to comply, and on November 26, 1789, he urged all Americans to "unite in most humbly offering our prayers and supplications to the great Lord and Ruler of Nations, and beseech him to pardon our national and other transgressions."[24]

There had been opposition, though. When the idea was proposed, Representative Thomas Tucker of South Carolina made a case that would be heard often in later American history. He argued that urging a day of thanksgiving and prayer "is a business with which Congress [can] have nothing to do; it is a religious matter, and, as such, is proscribed to us."[25] His colleagues did not agree, as we know, and the resolution passed despite his objections. The tragedy is that the very argument the First Congress dismissed as inconsistent with its meaning in the First Amendment has become the main interpretation of the First Amendment today.

It is even more ironic that the words of the First Congress would ever be used to oppose chaplains. Two days before the House of Representatives approved the final wording of the First Amendment, a statute providing for compensation for chaplains was enacted into law. The matter had been under discussion since earlier in the spring of 1789, when both the House and the Senate elected their chaplains. Clearly, the First Congress did not see the inconsistency some later Americans would between appointing chaplains and their intended meaning of the First Amendment. The reason for this is simple. The inconsistency doesn't exist.

It falls, then, to one of America's great legal minds to summarize this issue for us. Joseph Story was both an associate justice of the United States Supreme Court from 1811 until 1845 and a professor at Harvard Law School during many of the same years. Given that he was appointed to the bench by James Madison, that his *Commentaries on the Constitution* were the reference of record among early American lawyers, and that he helped to shape the nation's jurisprudence for nearly half a century, his understanding of the meaning of the First Amendment should be taken as definitive.

Probably at the time of the adoption of the Constitution, and of the amendment to it now under consideration [the First Amendment], the general if not the universal sentiment in America was that Christianity ought to receive encouragement from the State so far as was not incompatible with the private rights of conscience and the freedom of religious worship. An attempt to level all religions, and to make it a matter of state policy to hold all in utter indifference, would have created universal disapprobation, if not universal indignation.[26]

The real object of the First Amendment was not to countenance, much less to advance, Mahametanism, or Judaism, or infidelity, by prostrating Christianity; but to exclude all rivalry among Christian sects, and to prevent any national ecclesiastical establishment which should give to a hierarchy the exclusive patronage of the national government. It thus cut off the means of religious persecution (the vice and pest of former ages), and of the subversion of the rights of conscience in matters of religion which had been trampled upon almost from the days of the Apostles to the present age . . .[27]

2

OF CHEESE, WALLS, AND CHURCHES

It was New Year's morning in 1802, and Thomas Jefferson was standing in the door of the White House, eagerly awaiting his celebrated guest. The press would later report that Jefferson was wearing his usual black suit and respectable "Republican" shoes and that he was as nervously excited as anyone in the milling crowd that day.

It had taken the guest more than a month to reach Washington. Arriving on December 29 in a wagon drawn by six horses, the guest's trip by sloop and sleigh had been closely followed by the nation's newspapers. Everyone now knew that today the guest would be regally conveyed down Pennsylvania Avenue on a dray drawn by two horses. All Washington was astir with the news.

When the guest finally arrived at the White House, speeches were made. Jefferson heard himself celebrated as the man "the Supreme Ruler of the Universe had raised up to defend Republicanism and to baffle all the arts of Aristocracy." The president was gracious, offered words of welcome, and then stood ready for the guest to be presented.

"Sir," said the citizen appointed to make the introduction, "we have attempted to prove our love to our President, not in words alone, but in deeds and in truth. With this address we send you . . . a cheese."

And so it was. A cheese. The guest, as it turned out, was the largest, smelliest, most grotesque cheese the nation had ever seen. It measured more than four feet across, thirteen feet around, and it was seventeen inches high, gravity having done its worst. It weighed more than 1,235 pounds, was painted bright red, and boasted Jefferson's favorite motto: "Rebellion to tyrants is obedience to God."

It was presented, said the citizens who had created it, "as a peppercorn of the esteem which we bear to our Chief Magistrate, and as a sacrifice to Republicanism. It is not the last stone in the Bastille, nor is it of any great consequence as an article of worth, but, as a free-will offering, we hope it will be favorably received."

It could hardly be otherwise. The cheese had been lovingly made by the citizens of Cheshire, a small farming community in the Berkshire Hills of western Massachusetts. These were Baptist farmers, to be sure, and they had lived in the officially Congregationalist state of Massachusetts for so long and suffered such indignities that when Thomas Jefferson, champion of religious liberty, was elected president of the United States, these Baptist farmers could contain themselves no longer. Something had to be done. When news of Republican victory had reached the tiny community, the Baptist parson had effused, "Now the greatest orbit in America is occupied by the brightest orb." And the idea of the great cheese was born.

What a day it had been on the morning of July 20, 1801, when the Baptist families of Cheshire had converged on the farm of Elisha Brown Jr. to milk the more than nine hundred cows necessary to produce the mammoth cheese. And these were Republican cows, the good people of Cheshire later assured Mr. Jefferson. In fact, when the great cheese began to spoil many months after arriving in Washington, the citizens of Cheshire suspected that some Federalist cows had despicably contaminated the yield.

It didn't matter, though. On New Year's morning of 1802, all that filled the thoughts of the Baptists of Cheshire or anyone else on the White House lawn was that this was "the greatest Cheese in America, for the greatest Man in America."

Mr. Jefferson was indeed honored. He stammered his gratitude and leaned toward the cheese to fill his lungs with its scent—an act he quickly realized was unnecessary since the cheese had grown so strong that one reporter claimed it could have walked from Baltimore to Washington by itself.

Finally, shaking hands and making his apologies, Thomas Jefferson turned back into the White House. He rested, tended to the daily agenda, and before the day was done, he penned the words that would transform the role of religion in American public life.[1]

———

TRAVELERS WHO VISIT MONTICELLO, THOMAS JEFFERSON'S BELOVED home in the splendid hills of Albemarle County, Virginia, have an opportunity to view one of the most unusual gravestones in American history. It adorns the grave of Jefferson himself, and what makes the stone so remarkable are the words chiseled into it, the words the great man chose to define how history should remember him.

Here was buried
Thomas Jefferson
Author of the
Declaration of Independence
Of The
Statute of Virginia
For
Religious Freedom
And Father of The
University of Virginia
Born April 2, 1743 O.S.[2]
Died July 4, 1826

Those unfamiliar with Jefferson's life may find nothing strange about these words. Besides, if the man buried beneath was happy with them, why should anyone else be troubled? Yet the oddity has baffled minds throughout the nearly two centuries since Jefferson died, for they fail to mention that he was a governor of Virginia, a minister to France, a member of Congress, secretary of state under George Washington, vice president under John Adams, and, oh yes, the president of the United States.

There is probably no solving the mystery of Jefferson's omissions. Speculation has filled volumes through the years and scholars are no closer to agreement. Still, whatever else he may have intended by his unusual choice of words, it is clear that he regarded his statute for religious freedom as among his greatest accomplishments. Undoubtedly, he expected history to remember him for this particular contribution to liberty, and he may have sought to assure that remembrance by the words he placed on his gravestone. If so, he would certainly be surprised by the manner in which religion is most often connected to his memory today, for he is not primarily remembered for that Virginia statute on religion. Instead, his thoughts on religion are most commonly associated with a single phrase in a single sentence from a single letter written early in his presidency. It is a phrase that has become so familiar that many Americans believe it is found in the Constitution itself. It is the phrase "wall of separation between church and state."

Under normal circumstances, these words might have endured as little more than a guide to Jefferson's thoughts on religion in America. Later generations might have viewed them simply as a source of helpful insight, along with hundreds of other quotes by the founding fathers, into what the framers of the Bill of Rights meant by the First Amendment religion clauses. The words might even have been understood as representative of one phase of Jefferson's religious and political development.

Instead, in 1947, the United States Supreme Court made these seven words the law of the land in matters of religion. In the ruling of the Court, Jefferson's phrase became the very meaning of the first ten words of the First Amendment and yet with such a novel interpretation that Jefferson himself would have been amazed. Never before in American history had language from a private letter been elevated to such stature. Never before had a man's words been set at such odds with his life and given the authority of law. Never before had an action of State been interpreted exclusively through the words of a man who was not present at the time and who was writing more than a decade after the fact. The Court's use of Jefferson's phrase would prove to be an American tragedy, and little makes this more certain than the words and actions of Jefferson himself.

In October of 1801, the Baptist Association of Danbury, Connecticut, sent a letter to Thomas Jefferson. Their purpose was to congratulate Jefferson for his election to the presidency and celebrate him as a champion of religious liberty. The Baptists of Danbury, Connecticut—not unlike the cheese-making Baptists of Cheshire, Massachusetts—had endured much in an officially Congregationalist state. Jefferson was more than their choice as president. He was champion of their cause, a Republican knight contending manfully against Federalist oppressors.

Though the date on the manuscript was October 7, 1801, for some unexplained reason, the letter did not reach the president's desk until December 30. It is not hard to imagine Jefferson, then, contemplating the letter's contents as the New Year dawned and as the great cheese, sent for very much the same reasons as the Danbury letter, neared the nation's capitol.

The address of the Danbury Baptist Association,
in the State of Connecticut; assembled October 7th. AD 1801
To *Thomas Jefferson* Esq. President of the united States of America.

Sir,

Among the many millions in America and Europe who rejoice in your Election to office; we embrace the first opportunity which we have enjoy‚d in our collective capacity, since your Inauguration, to express our great satisfaction, in your appointment to the chief Magistracy in the United States: And though our mode of expression may be less courtly and pompous than what many others clothe their addresses with, we beg you, Sir to believe, that none are more sincere.

Our Sentiments are uniformly on the side of Religious Liberty—That Religion is at all times and places a Matter between God and Individuals—That no man ought to suffer in Name, person or effects on account his religious Opinions—That the legitimate Power of civil Government extends no further than to punish the man who *works ill to his neighbour:* But Sire. Our constitution of government is not specific. Our antient charter, together with the Laws made coincident therewith, were adopted as the Basis of our government, At the time of our revolution; and such had been our Laws & usages, & such still are: that Religion is consider‚d as the first object of Legislation; & therefore what religious privileges we enjoy (as a minor part of the State) we enjoy as favors granted, and not as inalienable rights: and these favors we receive at the expense of such degrading acknowledgements, as are inconsistent with the rights of the fre(e)men. It is not to be wondered at therefore; if those, who seek after *power & gain* under the pretence of *government & Religion* should reproach their fellow men—should reproach their chief Magistrate, as an enemy of religion Law & good order because he will not, dares not assume the prerogative of Jehovah and make Laws to govern the Kingdom of Christ.

Sir, we are sensible that the President of the united States, is not the national Legislator, & also sensible that the national government cannot destroy the Laws of each State; but our hopes are strong that the sentiments of our beloved President, which have had such genial

Effect already, like the radiant beams of the Sun, will shine & prevail through all these States and all the world till Hierarchy and Tyranny be destroyed from the Earth. Sir, when we reflect on your past services, and see a glow of philanthropy and good will shining forth in a course of more than thirty years we have reason to believe that America,s God has raised you up to fill the chair of State out of that good will which he bears to the Millions which you preside over. May God strengthen you for the arduous task which providence & the voice of the people have cal,d you to sustain and support you in your Administration against all the predetermine,d opposition of those who wish to rise to wealth & importance on the poverty and subjection of the people—

And may the Lord preserve you safe from every evil and bring you at last to his Heavenly Kingdom through Jesus Christ our Glorious Mediator.

Signed in behalf of the Association,

Neh,h Dodge   )

Ephm Robbins   )The Committee[3]

Stephen S. Nelson   )

The note, now so crucial to history, might easily have been discarded. Others of the kind certainly were. Jefferson received dozens like it and no one would have thought the worse of him had he failed to answer this one. Yet from time to time he remembered the opportunity such correspondence gave him for "sowing useful truths & principles among the people, which might germinate and become rooted among their political tenets."[4] In short, he thought he might do some good in answering this particular letter, and it also didn't hurt that his reply would land in the stronghold of his political enemies: the Federalists of New England. The day before he wrote it, he told his attorney general, Levi Lincoln, "I know it will give great offence to the New England clergy: but the advocate for religious freedom is to expect neither peace nor forgiveness from them."[5]

They are the words of a wounded man. Jefferson had suffered horrible criticism during his campaign for president, and the barbs had penetrated his sensitive soul. This was in part because Federalist attacks were often expressed in theological terms. Jefferson could not simply be an agnostic or a Unitarian; he was the anti-Christ, an agent of the "atheistical" French. The assaults did not subside when he took office, either. Because he refused to recommend days of prayer and fasting as his predecessors had done, the Federalists worked even harder to convince the public that the Jefferson administration signaled the end of God's blessing on America. The Danbury Baptists sought to console their champion, commending him for not presuming to "make Laws to govern the Kingdom of Christ" and associating their suffering under the Federalists with his own. Perhaps because of the welcome tone of comfort in the Danbury note as well as the opportunity to strike back at his enemies, Jefferson decided to grant a reply. He could not have guessed at its ultimate impact.

> To messrs. Nehemiah Dodge, Ephraim Robins, & Stephen S. Nelson, a committee of the Danbury Baptist association in the estate of Connecticut.
>
> Gentlemen
>
> The affectionate sentiments of esteem and approbation which you are so good as to express towards me, on behalf of the Danbury Baptist association, give me the highest satisfaction. my duties dictate a faithful & zealous pursuit of the interests of my constituents, & in proportion as they are persuaded of my fidelity to those duties, the discharge of them becomes more and more pleasing.
>
> Believing with you that religion is a matter which lies solely

between Man & his God, that he owes account to none other for his faith or his worship, that the legitimate powers of government reach actions only, & not opinions, I contemplate with sovereign reverence that act of the whole American people which declared that their legislature should "make no law respecting an establishment of religion, or prohibiting the free exercise thereof," thus building a *wall of separation between Church & State.* [emphasis added], adhering to this expression of the supreme will of the nation in behalf of the rights of conscience, I shall see with sincere satisfaction the progress of those sentiments which tend to restore to man all his natural rights, convinced he has no natural right in opposition to his social duties.

I reciprocate your kind prayers for the protection & blessing of the common father and creator of man, and tender you for yourselves & your religious association, assurances of my high respect & esteem.

Th: Jefferson

Jan. 1. 1802[6]

That seven words from this letter should become a defining principle of law is one of the great curiosities in the American history. Yet, even if the Supreme Court was right to grant the words such weight in the jurisprudence of the nation, the meaning of the words has been horribly mangled, and largely through a refusal to let their author speak for himself.

The problem modern Americans often have in understanding the political thoughts of their forefathers has to do with the issue of federalism. Today, it is common for a television newscaster to announce some action of the federal government by saying, for example, "The government issued a statement this morning . . ." Because of the prominence of the federal government in recent history, no one is confused by the reference. A member of the founding generation listening to the broadcast, though, would ask, "Which government? Is the announcer referring to the general or federal government? Or is it the government of a state? Perhaps the announcer means a county or territorial government. Then, of course, there is the government of a township or a city. Which of these governments does the announcer mean?"

When the founding generation of Americans turned to the business of creating a country, they had just fought a war against a centralized and controlling national government. They had no intention of creating an American version of the same evil. Finding themselves in need of a new constitution to replace the Articles of Confederation, the framers were careful to create a general or national government that would have only limited, delegated authority. They believed they could best assure their freedoms by investing primary authority in the states and only secondary, limited authority in the federal government. Through decentralization, they would slay the dragon of tyranny. So grave was their concern that the national government assume no more authority than was delegated by the states that they concluded the Bill of Rights with the clarifying Tenth Amendment.

> The powers not delegated to the United States by the Constitution, nor prohibited by it to the States, are reserved to the States respectively, or to the people.

Clearly, the states intended to jealously guard their authority and assure that the national government only assumed such authority, or powers, as the states granted it in the Constitution. This concern was paramount in the minds of the founders. The matter of the states being ultimate even expressed itself in the language of the day. Notice that in the Danbury Baptist Association's letter to Jefferson, the phrase "United States" is written as "united States," a clear attempt to signal that the national government was simply a limited merger of the states and not an entity unto itself. In fact, for decades after the framing of the Constitution, the words *United States* were always followed by a *plural* verb. One wouldn't say "the United States is." Rather, the language of early America was "the United States are." Always the federal government was understood as comprised of the states, limited by the states, and doing the bidding of the states.

This is vital to understanding Jefferson's metaphor in the Danbury letter. Later generations have read the letter in terms of the language of their day and have assumed that Jefferson believed the First Amendment erected a wall of separation between all government and all religion. This is a misunderstanding based on the assumption that the generic term *State* alluded to all government.

The author himself said otherwise. Jefferson clearly believed that the wall of separation was not between all government and all religion, but rather between the national or federal government and religion, leaving the states free to be as religious as they wanted to be. In a letter to Reverend Samuel Miller, one of the few Presbyterian clergymen to endorse his administration, Jefferson wrote:

> I consider the government of the United States as interdicted [forbidden] by the Constitution from intermeddling with religious institutions, their doctrines, discipline, or exercise. This results not only from the provision that no law shall be made respecting the establishment or free exercise of religion but from that also which reserves to the States the powers not delegated to the United States. Certainly no power to prescribe any religious exercise, or to assume authority in religious discipline, has been delegated to the General Government. *It must then rest with the states, as far as it can be in any human authority.*[7] (emphasis added)

Such views were not reserved for private remarks in obscure letters alone. So intense was the public pressure Jefferson felt against his refusal to declare national days of thanksgiving and prayer that he addressed the matter in his second inaugural address. Delivered in March of 1805, the speech is essential to understanding the Danbury letter since it treats, at least in part, the same issues but two years later in Jefferson's administration.

> In matters of religion, I have considered that its free exercise is placed by the constitution independent of the powers of the general [federal] government. I have therefore undertaken, on no occasion, to prescribe the religious exercises suited to it; but have left them, as the constitution found them, under the direction and discipline of State or Church authorities acknowledged by the several religious societies.[8]

Jefferson obviously believed that the states had authority in matters of religion that the Constitution denied to the federal government. He thought the same way about other First Amendment freedoms. In an 1804 letter to Abigail Adams, Jefferson wrote, "While we deny that Congress have a right to control the freedom of the press, we have ever asserted the right of the States, and their exclusive right, to do so."[9]

This view, which some scholars have called a "jurisdictional interpretation"—meaning that both the First Amendment and Jefferson's wall metaphor define federal as opposed to state jurisdiction in the matter of religion—was not unique to Jefferson. In fact, it was the law of the land. In 1833, Chief Justice John Marshall, writing for a united Court in *Barron v. City Council of Baltimore*, stated that freedoms guaranteed in the Bill of Rights "contain no expression indicating an intention to apply them to the state governments."[10] Later, in *Permoli v. Municipality No. 1 of the City of New Orleans*, the Supreme Court ruled that "[t]he Constitution makes no provision for protecting the citizens of the respective States in their religious liberties; this is left to the state constitutions and laws."[11] Summarizing this early American consensus, Justice Joseph Story explained that the purpose of the First Amendment was to "exclude from the national government all power to act upon the subject of religion."[12] In addition, "the whole power over the subject of religion is left exclusively to the state government, to be acted upon according to their own sense of justice, and the state constitutions."[13]

When Thomas Jefferson wrote to the Danbury Baptist Association that the First Amendment erected a wall of separation between church and state, he was saying no more than the founding generation believed. Fearing a national religion enforced by a centralized government, the framers of the First Amendment had forbidden the federal government from passing any law that would create an established religion, meaning a State religion or a national church. For Jefferson, this meant that a president should not even call for days of prayer and thanksgiving. For other presidents—like Washington, Adams, and Madison—it did not. For all of that generation, though, the understanding was certain that the states were permitted to establish religion or support religion as aggressively as the people allowed. This was the glory of American federalism in regard to religious freedom. Thus, even if the Supreme Court of 1947 was right to put so much weight on seven words from Jefferson's letter to the Danbury Baptists—and it was not—it was wrong to interpret them as a ban on all government touching any matter of religion in American society.

It is obvious from what we have seen that Thomas Jefferson's meaning in the Danbury letter is best understood when Jefferson speaks for himself. Let us not muzzle him now, then. Though it certainly would have been wiser for the Supreme Court not to choose one sentence among millions by one founding father among dozens in order to interpret the First Amendment, let us continue to use Jefferson as an illustration of what the founding generation intended.

Yet we must be wise. What the Court forgot when it invoked

Jefferson was how men change. We must not make the same error. Heraclites was right when he said that no man can set his foot in the same river twice because both the man and the river change. Men do indeed change. They mature, adapt, transform. Their views in youth are not the same as in old age, and there are a thousand variations along the way. No one stage of life summarizes the whole of the man.

For example, which is the true Abraham Lincoln? Is it the man who in the early days of his presidency was willing to keep slavery in place if it meant the Union could be saved?[14] Or is it the older, more haggard man—who had endured the death of a son and the gnashing steel of war—proclaiming in his Second Inaugural Address that slavery was a national sin that God intended to cleanse?

Which is the true Winston Churchill? Was it the brash and atheistic subaltern in India who eschewed revealed religion? Or was it the scared prisoner of war in South Africa years later who found himself in danger during an escape attempt and reclaimed the Christian faith of his youth?

And which is the true Ronald Reagan? Is it the Democrat actor who voted for Franklin Roosevelt or the Republican statesman who spent his latter years dismantling Roosevelt's legacy?

The fact is that every phase of a man's life is part of the pattern of the whole and should be considered as a window into the truth of his life. Of few men is this more true than Jefferson. He was not as fixed in his opinions as the Supreme Court has stated. He grew; he climbed; he renewed. If Jefferson is to become the icon of religion in early America, then let the whole of Jefferson come into play.

There is little question that in the 1770s and 1780s, Thomas Jefferson was a deist for whom traditional religion held little attraction. He believed, as he wrote in his *Notes on the State of Virginia*, that religion had social value "sufficient to preserve peace and order."[15] Beyond this, though, his Jesus was a great moral teacher, his Bible was so much of human fabrication as to demand editing, and his faith was solely in the moral perfectibility of man. In truth, Jefferson viewed Christianity as little more than the best moral system surviving from antiquity.

Yet, even in this stage of rationalistic religion, Jefferson repeatedly encouraged government support for religion. When American independence became official in July of 1776, each colony found itself in need of new laws to replace the legal codes of England. Virginia looked to Thomas Jefferson, as it often did, to head a committee intended to "revise, alter, amend, repeal, or introduce all or any of the said laws" of the Commonwealth.[16] As assignments were made and work parceled out among the various members of the committee, Jefferson ended up with responsibility for drafting the bills related to religion (see appendix 2). The most famous of these bills was known as the Bill for Establishing Religious Freedom and was passed by the Virginia House of Delegates in December of 1785.

This was Jefferson's opportunity to write his Enlightenment-inspired love of religious liberty into the laws of Virginia. He did so with such passion that his soaring phrases are among those by which later generations have most remembered him: "Almighty God hath created the mind free"; "our civil rights have no dependence on our religious opinions, any more than our opinions in physics or geometry"; "the opinions of man are not the object of civil government, nor under its jurisdiction"; "truth is great and will prevail if left to herself; that she is the proper and sufficient antagonist to error."

Were there no more to the story, the picture might seem complete: Jefferson the Enlightenment rationalist writes a law to free his fellow Virginians from the tyranny of State religion. Yet there is indeed a larger picture. The bill known as the Virginia Bill for Establishing Religious Freedom, of which Jefferson was so proud that he included it in the list of accomplishments on his tombstone, was but one bill, Number 82, among a long list of bills fashioned for the laws of

Virginia. It was the first of five bills that Jefferson authored on religion, and it is the one best remembered because it was the broadest in application, was written in near poetic terms, and, of course, because Jefferson wished to be remembered for it.

The other four bills Jefferson authored lead to very different conclusions about his views and yet conclusions completely consistent with his "wall of separation" metaphor if rightly understood. Bill Number 83, for example, was entitled "A Bill for Saving the Property of the Church Heretofore by Law Established" and was designed to protect the property rights of the Anglican Church. Bill Number 84 was designed to protect worship and even included fines for Sabbath breaking. Bill Number 85 was entitled "A Bill for Appointing Days of Public Fasting and Thanksgiving," something Jefferson would refuse to do as president but had no objection to when suggested by the state. Finally, Bill Number 86 was entitled "A Bill for Annulling Marriages Prohibited by the Levitical Law," which not only annulled marriages inconsistent with Levitical law but fined couples found cohabitating.

Obviously, though in this phase of his life Jefferson did not hold to the supernatural claims of Christianity, he did work for Christianity's moral impact on society. This was completely in keeping with his view of the First Amendment, which he understood as forbidding a national religion yet permitting states to enforce religion widely, even to the extent of mandating Sabbaths and defining marriage in biblical terms as he had done in Virginia.

It was also during this more deistic phase of his life that Jefferson encouraged religion while he served as president. This is hard to reconcile with his stated intention to leave religion to the states and deny any religious influence to the federal government. It is no less true for being inconsistent, though, and it does confirm again that Jefferson never envisioned a completely secular state, even during his years of religious skepticism.

In 1803, Jefferson recommended to Congress the passage of a treaty that provided a stipend of $100 annually to support a Catholic priest in ministering to the Kaskaskia Indians.[17] Similar treaties were enacted with his endorsement for the Wyandot Indians and other tribes in 1806 and the Cherokee in 1807. Another act that originated in 1787 ordained special lands "for the sole use of Christian Indians" and reserved land for the Moravian Brethren "for civilizing the Indians and promoting Christianity." When this act was renewed, it bore the title "An Act regulating the grants of land appropriated for Military services and for the Society of the United Brethren for propagating the Gospel among the Heathen." Three times during his administration, Congress extended this act and Jefferson signed it into law. Not once did he even consider vetoing it on the basis that it violated the First Amendment or his own "wall of separation" metaphor.[18]

This was Jefferson in the years of Deism. Then a change came over him. As Yale historian and chief of the Manuscript Division at the Library of Congress, James H. Hutson, has explained:

> Scholars believe that, as a result of reading, sometime around 1793, Joseph Priestley's *An History of the Corruptions of Christianity*, Jefferson experienced a "conversion" to Unitarian Christianity. Priestley's book "amounted almost to a revelation" to Jefferson because it argued—and proved to his satisfaction—that the teachings of Christianity that he found unintelligible and, therefore, unacceptable were additions to and distortions of Christ's original message, foisted off on the faithful over the centuries by self interested clerics. Christ's real message, according to Priestley, was not much more than a simple, demystified system of morality that was consistent with Jefferson's own conception of what a true religion ought to be. Priestley's book persuaded Jefferson that he was a Christian after all and henceforth he was not reluctant to proclaim the fact to friends.[19]

From the time of this "conversion" on, Jefferson spoke differently of his faith. "I am a Christian," he wrote a friend, "in the only sense in which he [Jesus] wished anyone to be."[20] "I am a real Christian," he wrote another, "a disciple of the doctrines of Jesus."[21]

The tale of Jefferson's subsequent journey of faith is fascinating and warrants further study than it has received. For our purposes in understanding how Jefferson viewed the role of religion and government, though, the entire tale is not relevant. Still, there is one feature of Jefferson's spiritual life that so challenges prevailing interpretations of religion and State in early America that it must be treated at length here.

Once Jefferson began pursuing his minimalist Christianity, he also began attending church. This alone is not remarkable. Where he went to church is remarkable, though, for Thomas Jefferson regularly attended worship services in the House of Representatives.

It will come as a shock to Americans raised on an assumed national history of wide separation between church and state that a church might meet in a federal building. Yet, as Hutson contends, "It is no exaggeration to say that, on Sundays in Washington during Thomas Jefferson's presidency, the state became the church."[22]

Worship services had actually begun in the nation's Capitol before the federal government moved to Washington in the fall of 1800. As early as July 2, 1795, the *Federal Orrery*, a Boston newspaper, reported:

City of Washington, June 19. It is with much pleasure that we discover the rising consequence of our infant city. Public worship is now regularly administered at the Capitol, every Sunday morning, at 11 o'clock by the Reverend Mr. Ralph.[23]

One possible explanation for the use of the Capitol as a church may be in the lack of other churches in Washington. As late as 1803,

US Senator John Quincy Adams complained, "There is no church of any denomination in this city."[24] In fact, churches did not proliferate in Washington until many years after its founding. "For several years after the seat of government was fixed at Washington," one citizen of the time reported, "there were but two small [wooden] churches . . . Now, in 1837, there are 22 churches of brick or stone."[25]

Regardless of the reason church services were first held in the Capitol building, once begun they continued there until 1866 when the First Congregational Church of Washington used the House chambers for both church and Sunday school. This means that church services were held in the House of Representatives for the first seventy years of American history. There is no indication that the practice was ever thought controversial, and this, of course, confirms that general support for religion while avoiding a national religion was the constitutional balancing act that early America achieved.

It is not insignificant that Jefferson first attended church in the House of Representatives two days after he wrote the Danbury letter suggesting that the First Amendment erected a "wall of separation between church and state." He penned the famous reply on Friday, January 1, 1802. On Sunday, January 3, "contrary to all former practice," he went to his first church service in the House, which he attended "constantly" for the next seven years. [26] Certainly, whatever his meaning in the "wall of separation" metaphor, it could not have included a ban on government support for religion, or Jefferson himself could not have in good conscience attended church in the House of Representatives just two days later and for the remainder of his presidency.

There is little doubt he found a beloved spiritual home in the Capitol church. An early Washington insider reported that "Jefferson during his whole administration, was a most regular attendant. The seat he chose the first day Sabbath, and the adjoining one, which his private secretary occupied, were ever afterwards by the courtesy of the congregation, left for him."[27] He became a fixture at the meetings and gained a reputation for attending even through violent weather. Stories circulated about encounters with the president at church, as in the tale told in 1806 by Catharine Mitchill, the wife of a New York senator, who stepped on Jefferson's foot while leaving a service. "I became so prodigiously frighten'd," she recounted, "that I could not stop to make an apology."[28]

The happenings at the Capitol church filled the journals that early Americans were fond of keeping. John Quincy Adams, who was a US senator while Jefferson was in the White House, often mentioned the church in journals he kept during his years in Washington. "Attended public service at the Capitol where Mr. Rattoon, an Episcopalian clergyman from Baltimore preached a sermon," noted one entry.[29] "Religious service is usually performed on Sundays at the Treasury office and at the Capitol. I went both forenoon and afternoon to the Treasury," reported another.[30]

Many visitors to the Capitol church remembered the press of the crowd and the difficulty of finding a seat. One congressman reported, "Attended in the morning at the Capitol . . . very full assembly. Many of the Members present."[31] Another remembered that "the floor of the House offered insufficient space, the platform behind the Speaker's chairs, and every spot where a chair could be wedged in" was filled.[32] Apparently, the crowds never abated. By 1857, when the House moved into its new home in the extension, more than two thousand people were attending church there every week.[33]

Jefferson's experiences at the Capitol church are fascinating to observe from the distance of centuries. A British diplomat reported that during Jefferson's administration, "A Presbyterian, sometimes a Methodist, a member of the Church of England, or a Quaker, sometimes even a woman took the Speaker's chair," which was used as a pulpit.[34] The woman was almost certainly Dorothy Ripley, the first female to conduct religious services in the House and probably the first to speak in Congress under any circumstances. Ripley was English and had crossed the Atlantic nineteen times to preach to American audiences. Jefferson heard her and was not scandalized at a woman preacher.

He heard sermons on the Second Coming, on how the nation would fail because its officials violated the Sabbath, on profanity, on the need to be born again, and on how the Millennium would begin in America, to name but a few topics. He also sat through an impromptu sermon from the gallery given by a Quaker woman, the tears of overheated evangelists, and a two-hour homily by a Catholic priest who had promised to speak briefly on a few informal thoughts.

He must have thought well of it all. He even tried to help and ordered the Marine Band to play for the services. They proved ostentatious and were never scheduled again. He then approved churches in the War Office and the Treasury building, with the latter gaining a reputation for more "religious" services because communion was served there. In time, a church began to meet in the Supreme Court's chambers, which were also in the Capitol building. This was probably welcomed by Chief Justice John Marshall, who was the vice president of the American Bible Society.

There is an anecdote that captures better than any other on record the approach to religion that moved Thomas Jefferson to faithfully attend his church in the House of Representatives. He was walking to church on Sunday "with his large red prayer book under his arm" when a friend happened upon him. It was the Reverend Ethan Allen.

"Which way are you walking, Mr. Jefferson?" Allen asked.

"To Church, Sir."

"You? Going to Church, Mr. J? You do not believe a word in it!"

"Sir," said Mr. Jefferson, "no nation has ever yet existed or been governed without religion. Nor can be. The Christian religion is the best religion that has been given to man and I as chief Magistrate of this nation am bound to give it the sanction of my example. Good morning, Sir."[35]

James Hutson, whose valuable work has helped to keep the knowledge of the Capitol church alive in our time, has summarized the meaning of Jefferson's experience there:

> By attending church services in Congress, Jefferson intended to send to the nation the strongest symbol possible that he was a friend of religion, hoping thereby to retain the political support of pious New England republicans who might be misled by the compromising sound of the "wall of separation" metaphor in his letter to their Danbury brethren into believing the slanders of his implacable opponents that he was an infidel or worse. On a policy level, Jefferson used the wall of separation metaphor in the sense of a wall of segmentation, as a partition demarcating the religious activities the government could and could not support. In this view, the government could not be a party to any attempt to impose upon the country a uniform religious exercise or observance; it could, on the other hand, support, as being in the public interest voluntary, non-discriminatory religious activity, including church services, by putting at its disposal public property, public facilities, and public personnel, including the president himself.[36]

It has been necessary to deal at length with Jefferson's connection to the church that met in the US House of Representatives because it is the ultimate statement of challenge to the contemporary understanding of both Jefferson and the founding generation's view of church and state. Clearly, the man whose language has become the governing principle of the church/state relationship in America today held nothing like the views that have been ascribed to him. Thomas

Jefferson may not have been traditional or orthodox in his religious views. This is, for our purposes here, beside the point. He was, though, completely at ease with federal and state support for religion as long as a national religion was never attempted.

If the courts today wish to erect, as the *Everson* Court said, "a high and impregnable" wall of separation between church and state, they may do it by fiat, but they cannot legitimately base such a construction on the life or words of Thomas Jefferson. Indeed, the Court made a critical error when it invoked Jefferson in support of a secular State. Through ignorance of the truth, it has instead invoked a man whose life is at odds with the very society the Court sought to produce.

3

THE TURNING

His name was Father James Coyle, and he was the very image of the Irish Catholic priest, complete with mischievous smile and heavy brogue. Born in Ireland and ordained in Rome in 1896, he had begun his ministry in Mobile, Alabama, first in a parish and then in a school for boys. When an older priest died an untimely death in 1904, the bishop of Mobile appointed Father Coyle as pastor of Birmingham's St. Paul's Cathedral. He would serve there for the next seventeen years of his life.

There were easier places for a Catholic priest to minister. Birmingham was a notorious hotbed of anti-Catholic rage. But then Birmingham in those days was filled with a great deal of rage—toward Jews, toward Catholics, and most of all toward blacks. In fact, Birmingham then was a difficult place for anyone who wasn't white, Protestant, and a member of the Ku Klux Klan. Father Coyle seemed free of fear, though. He regularly wrote letters to the newspapers defending Catholicism and despite death threats sat on his porch in the evenings with his prayer book and rosary, waving to the passing cars.

It is likely that Father Coyle knew the Reverend Edwin Stephenson only casually. St. Paul's was not far from the Jefferson County Courthouse where Stephenson made his living helping couples obtain marriage licenses and performing brief wedding ceremonies for a modest fee. Stephenson, a former barber, was a Methodist, a rabid anti-Catholic, and a member of the Ku Klux Klan.

The lives of these two men intersected violently on August 11, 1921. That afternoon, Father Coyle was visited by a Spanish laborer and a girl named Ruth whom Coyle knew was Reverend Stephenson's daughter. She had tried to become a Catholic some years before, but her staunchly Protestant father had stopped her. She attended, when she could escape her parents, another Catholic church in town called Our Lady of Sorrows. Earlier on this day the couple had tried to find the priest at the other church because they wished to be married. Frustrated, they crossed town to find Father Coyle and see if he would perform the ceremony. He said he would. After the proper questions and the summoning of witnesses, the sacrament was performed and the couple departed in the warm August sun to celebrate their love.

It was hours later that the tragedy occurred. Stephenson and his wife, frantic with suspicion that Catholics had kidnapped their daughter, were searching the streets, stopping cars, and begging the police to act. When little happened to their satisfaction, Stephenson decided it was time to confront Father Coyle, whom he was sure played some role in the matter. Coyle was, as usual in the evenings, sitting on the porch of his rectory, enjoying the cooling breeze of evening and the passersby. Though the details are uncertain to this day, apparently an enraged Stephenson approached Coyle and asked about his daughter. The two men argued loudly. Coyle admitted that he had married Ruth to a man named Pedro Gussman that afternoon. "You have married her to that nigger?" Stephenson charged. "You have treated me like a dirty dog." Tempers flared. Father Coyle charged Stephenson with being "a heretical bastard." Stephenson screamed a response, Father Coyle retorted in an Irish rage, and though it is not clear whether blows were exchanged, Stephenson produced a pistol and fired a bullet through the priest's brain. Within an hour, Father Coyle was dead, Stephenson was in jail in the same courthouse where he performed marriages, and Birmingham was ablaze with the news.

Then came the lawyer. He was young, gifted, and ambitious. Though not a member of the Klan, he had their confidence, and this is what landed him in the role of lead counsel for the defense of Edwin Stephenson.

The trial began on October 17 and was, by all accounts, a demonstration of Klan control of justice in Alabama at the time. The judge, four of the five defense lawyers, the Birmingham police chief, and most of the jurors were members of the Klan.

The lawyer knew how to play to Klan sympathies. His favorite tactic was to maneuver witnesses into admitting that they were Catholics. This, the lawyer knew, was all he needed to discredit their testimony in the eyes of the largely Klan jury.

Race as well as religion filled each question. At one point the lawyer arranged for the lights to be dimmed and then asked Pedro Gussman into the courtroom. When he asked witnesses whether they thought the man was black, all agreed that the Spaniard was a Negro. While Gussman himself was on the stand, the lawyer began discussing his hair. He had straightened it, hadn't he? Was he sure? A picture in the paper showed curls. Where were those curls now? The tactic was obvious to all. The lawyer's intent was to show Gussman as a "nigger ashamed of his race."

In his closing statement, the lawyer continued to raise the issue of Gussman's race. The prosecution had mentioned the man's "proud Castilian descent." The lawyer retorted in his closing that if Gussman was Castilian, "he has descended a long way."

Finally, in terms coded for Klan consumption, the lawyer proclaimed, "If the eyes of the world are upon the verdict of this jury, I would write that verdict in words that cannot be misunderstood, that the homes of the people of Birmingham cannot be touched. If that brings disgrace, God hasten the disgrace."

Years later, the head of the Klan in Alabama—who had earlier raised funds for Stephenson's defense—admitted that the Klan "didn't have much trouble winning that verdict." Stephenson left the courtroom a free man and immediately became an honored guest at Klan rallies around the state before settling back into his work as the marrying parson of the Jefferson County Courthouse.

It is the lawyer who fascinates. Less than a year after the Stephenson trial, he joined the Klan. One of his biographers said that he "placed his left hand over his heart, palm downward in a Fascist-like salute, raised his right straight to heaven, and repeated the Klan oath" before a rally of twenty-five thousand. Then, two years later, his ambitions moved him to renounce his Klan membership. He had greater things in mind.

It would help to know the lawyer's name. It was Hugo LaFayette Black, and in 1926 he was elected to the United States Senate. Slightly more than a decade later, President Franklin Roosevelt appointed him to the United States Supreme Court.

Then, in 1947, with a surprising reputation as a stridently liberal, even reactionary judge, Hugo Black wrote the majority opinion—the reasoning behind the Court's ruling—in *Everson v. Board of Education*. The ruling was an astonishing attempt to uproot a planting of faith that had survived for a century and a half, and it left Klansmen throughout the nation scratching their heads that Hugo Black had ever been theirs.[1]

A SUPREME COURT RULING IS RARELY THE PRODUCT OF ONE individual's thinking alone, but it is possible for one man to be the ruling spirit of the Court's doctrine on a specific issue, and this certainly was the case when Hugo Black wrote the majority opinion in *Everson v. Board of Education*. It is one of the most troubling rulings in the Court's history, and this may well be because it was written by one of the most troubling justices in the Court's history.

Franklin Roosevelt appointed Hugo Black to the Supreme Court because he had been impressed with Black's senatorial career. During his decade in the Senate, Black championed New Deal legislation and fought aggressively for organized labor. This pleased Roosevelt, who nominated the outspoken Southern senator in 1937 to fill the first Supreme Court vacancy of his administration.

Embarrassment followed. Shortly after Black's nomination, news of his Klan history spilled into the nation's newspapers, complete with photostatic copies of confirming documents. A media firestorm of the kind the nation had seldom seen erupted, and Black was widely urged to resign before he had even taken his seat on the Court. To answer his critics and assuage Roosevelt's humiliation, Black made an eleven-minute radio address that became the second most heard broadcast in history after Edward VIII's abdication speech of the year before. It worked. Black explained his Klan membership in terms most Americans living in the 1920s would understand. Three days later, he took his seat with the eight other justices of the United States Supreme Court.

During his first month on the court, Black told a friend, "When I joined the Klan, it was not anti-Catholic or anti-Jewish. With other progressive Democrats, I went in to prevent it from falling into the hands of machine politicians. We succeeded and I quit when I saw the Klan was going in the wrong direction."[2] This, of course, was a lie. The Klan had been anti-Catholic and anti-Jewish long before Black joined, yet the fact that the Klan was violently anti-Negro should have been justification enough for Black to avoid it altogether. The more likely reason for Black's membership was as he said twenty years after his confirmation: "If you wanted to be elected to the Senate in Alabama in the 1920s, you'd join the Klan too."[3]

Though Black became the most influential member of the Court during the two decades after World War II, his early years were a disappointment to some of his fellow justices. He routinely worked fourteen-hour days but the results were mediocre. His opinions sounded like Senate speeches and were unevenly reasoned. Justice Harlan Fiske Stone complained about Black openly to members of the press and even wrote Felix Frankfurter at Harvard Law School suggesting that he give Black some needed tutoring. It was a humiliating start for the senator from Alabama.

In time, Black would find his stride, but many suspected his career was fueled by his eagerness to live down his racist past. As one scholar has said, "The nagging question is not what Black's motivations in fact were in 1923, but what effect a lifetime of guilt had on his judicial career."[4] Perhaps it is this matter of guilt and a destabilizing anxiousness to appear broadminded that led to his uneven judicial philosophy. He strained to secure liberties for African-Americans, for example, but then wrote the majority opinion in *Korematsu v. United States*, the ruling that sent some 120,000 Japanese-Americans into detention centers during World War II. He stood with an unswerving free speech majority in the famous Pentagon Papers case and yet burned all of his conference notes and most of the materials in his case files before he died. Known for carrying a copy of the Constitution in his pocket, his final years on the bench gained him a reputation as a reactionary liberal who labored to unchain himself from constitutional restraint on his opinions.

A perfect example of Hugo Black's troubling judicial performance is his majority opinion in *Everson v. Board of Education*. Though it is a case upon which dozens of other religion cases have been decided, it is riddled with weak appeal to precedent, flawed historiography, and inconsistency of reasoning seldom found in a seminal Supreme Court ruling. In short, it is the single case upon which the role of religion in American public life turns, and yet it makes the reader wish that Justice Black had received the tutoring Justice Stone once recommended.

The facts of the *Everson* case are simple and illustrate one of the certain truths of history: that great events—like great men—often rise from insignificant beginnings. In 1941, the New Jersey legislature passed a statute authorizing "local school districts to make rules and contracts for the transportation of children to and from school."[5] To fulfill the intent of this statute, the Township of Ewing, New Jersey, passed a resolution that authorized reimbursement to parents for money they spent sending their children to public or Catholic parochial school "on regular buses operated by the public transportation system."[6]

A citizen of Ewing by the name of Arch Everson filed a lawsuit to stop the practice. He had two complaints. First, he claimed that New Jersey was using public funds for a private purpose and was therefore depriving him of his property without due process of law, and, second, he claimed that New Jersey was forcing him and others to pay taxes to support the Catholic Church, a violation in his opinion of the New Jersey and United States Constitutions. Everson lost on appeal to New Jersey's highest court—which held that neither the state nor the federal Constitutions were violated—and he decided to take his case to the US Supreme Court.

The Supreme Court dismissed Everson's first complaint immediately. He had argued that he was being taxed to provide a benefit he did not enjoy himself. The Court had dealt with this issue in 1930, though, and ruled in a case called *Cochran v. Louisiana State Board of Education* that it is indeed constitutional to tax people who do not receive direct benefit from that tax.[7]

The Court then turned its attention to the First Amendment aspect of Everson's case. After reviewing some of the horrors of religious oppression and the early American battle for religious liberty, largely in Virginia, Justice Black concluded the Court's ruling with two paragraphs that disconnected much that came afterward in American society from the intentions of the founders of America:

The "establishment of religion" clause of the First Amendment means at least this: Neither a state nor the Federal Government can set up a church. Neither can pass laws which aid one religion, aid all religions, or prefer one religion over another. Neither can force nor influence a person to go to or to remain away from church against his will or force him to profess a belief or disbelief in any religion. No person can be punished for entertaining or professing religious beliefs or disbeliefs, for church attendance or non-attendance. No tax in any amount, large or small, can be levied to support any religious activities or institutions, whatever they may be called, or whatever form they may adopt to teach or practice religion. Neither a state nor the Federal Government can, openly or secretly, participate in the affairs of any religious organizations or groups and vice versa. In the words of Jefferson, the clause against establishment of religion by law was intended to erect "a wall of separation between church and State."

* * *

The First Amendment has erected a wall between church and state. That wall must be kept high and impregnable. We could not approve the slightest breach.[8]

There is much in this language that every sincere lover of liberty can affirm. No one committed to freedom would force a man to attend a church against his will or keep him from the church of his choice, punish him for his beliefs or lack of beliefs, or wish the government to endorse one religion over another. Nor were any of these matters in question in the *Everson* case.

However, when the Court ruled that neither the state nor the federal government may aid religion in general, use tax revenues in any amount to support religion, or participate in the affairs of any religion or religious organization, it was doing nothing less than refashioning the religious life of the nation according to an unworkable, secularist vision.

Consider what this ruling might have meant had it been instantly obeyed in 1947. Beginning with the very building in which the justices sat, the figure of Moses holding the two tablets of the Ten Commandments would have been removed, and the words that signaled the opening of Court business—"God save the United States and this Honorable court"—would have required immediate editing. In the US Capitol, the Rotunda paintings of the baptism of Pocahontas and of George Washington ascending into heaven would have been removed, as would several other similar paintings, dozens of inscriptions mentioning God, and numerous statues of clergymen like Reverend Peter Muhlenberg, Reverend Roger Williams, and Reverend Marcus Whiteman. More importantly, congressional chaplains would have been instantly dismissed, the prayer before each session of Congress would have been suspended, and bills providing for the support of religion in any form would have been revoked.

At the Library of Congress, statues of Moses and the apostle Paul would have been removed and dozens of biblical references would have been chiseled from the walls. At Union Station, offending sentences like "The truth shall make you free" (John 8:32) and "Thou has put all things under his feet" (Psalm 8:6) would have been removed from statuary. This would only be the beginning. Thousands of biblical references, religious symbols, and images of religious leaders would have been removed throughout the nation's capital, including the phrase *Laus Deo* ("Praise be to God") that adorns the platinum cap atop the Washington Monument and the references to God in Thomas Jefferson's own words at the Jefferson Memorial.

The Pentagon would have begun scrambling to terminate its chaplaincy program in all the branches of the military, cease the printing of Bibles and religious materials, end chapel services at all of its service academies, and close all of its chapels at all of its installations around the world. Oaths, uniforms, and the very wording of the American military's mission in the world would have required immediate revision. It would have cost millions of dollars and required years to achieve, but it would have only been the beginning.

Because the *Everson* ruling applied to the states as well as the federal government, prayer, chaplaincy programs, religious inscriptions, and any legislation supportive of religion would have ended immediately at state houses around the country. Prayer would have ended in every school district in the nation, as would any religious content in textbooks, any religious inscriptions on school walls, and any religiously oriented programs on school property. A scouring of every state park, federal park, or even county playground for religious language and symbols would have been necessary. Moreover, any faith-oriented program in a prison, among law enforcement officers, in city or county governments, or in any even partially tax-supported organization would have had to end.

The *Everson* ruling called for the complete destruction of any connection between any level of government and any expression of religion anywhere in the country. This was new, radical, unintended by the founding fathers, un-envisioned by the American people, and virtually impossible to accomplish.

Moreover, it was simply bad law. To begin with, after thousands of words establishing a basis for the widest possible separation between religion and government, the Court then upheld the New Jersey practice of providing funds for the transportation of children to religious schools. In the final words of the decision, Justice Black wrote, "The First Amendment has erected a wall between church and state. That wall must be kept high and impregnable. We could not approve the slightest breach. New Jersey has not breached it here." The ruling is almost incomprehensible. Church and state must never touch, the

Court said, but the government of Ewing, New Jersey, may pay for transporting children to church schools. This conclusion was so at odds with the reasoning that came before it that both of the dissents in the case agreed with Justice Black's argument for wide separation of church and state but disagreed with his ultimate ruling.

Equally confusing was Justice Black's insistence upon the assumption that "the First Amendment has erected a wall between church and state." This had not been established as a matter of law. Only once before had the Court ever referred to Jefferson's "wall of separation" metaphor, and that was in an 1878 case called *Reynolds v. United States* that dealt with Mormon polygamy. Yet in *Reynolds* the Court had not ruled that the meaning of the establishment clause and Jefferson's "wall of separation" were the same. It had only mentioned the phrase as a matter of history. When Justice Black stated that the First Amendment erected a wall between church and state, he was rewriting history and stating as law what had never before been determined by the Court.

Let us remember that Thomas Jefferson was not present when the Constitution and the Bill of Rights were framed. He was the American ambassador to France. Also, he wrote the Danbury letter containing the "wall of separation" metaphor nearly a decade and a half after the First Amendment was written. Moreover, Justice Black used Jefferson's words in a way Jefferson's own life and politics do not support. It was Jefferson, after all, who approved funds for evangelizing Native Americans. It was Jefferson who attended church on federal property for most of his administration, approved still other churches on federal property, and even ordered the marine band to play in his church. It was also Jefferson who believed that the federal government was forbidden from establishing religion but that the state governments were not, as we have seen. Clearly, Justice Black used Jefferson's words in a manner that Jefferson himself would have opposed.

Yet let us take this even further. Let us assume for the sake of argument that Thomas Jefferson was a thorough-going secularist who intended his "wall of separation" phrase in the Danbury letter as a call for a completely nonreligious nation. This is clearly untrue, but let us grant it to make a point. There are still two vital questions raised by Justice Black's approach to history in *Everson*.

First, why did the Court focus on Jefferson's phrase and not on the congressional debates that produced the First Amendment to begin with? Never does Justice Black mention the debates over the wording of the First Amendment that we examined in the last chapter. Never is a case built from the intentions of the First Amendment's framers. Yet Jefferson's phrase is taken as the sole key to interpreting the First Amendment's meaning. This is despite the fact that for the months from June 7 to September 25, 1789, when some ninety founding fathers were debating the language of the First Amendment, there is not one mention of the phrase "separation of church and state" recorded in the *Congressional Record*. Certainly, if the purpose of the words, "Congress shall make no law respecting an establishment of religion" was to "erect a wall of separation between church and state," this would have received some mention during four months of debate.

A second question that must be asked is, why this focus on Jefferson? There were fifty-five men who framed the Constitution, and ninety were involved in the first federal Congress that framed the First Amendment and the Bill of Rights. Allowing for the overlap of nineteen individuals who were at both the Constitutional Convention and the first Congress, there were 126 founding fathers who framed the Constitution and the Bill of Rights. Thomas Jefferson was not among them, yet his words alone now govern the meaning of the First Amendment in American jurisprudence. Perhaps this is because Jefferson is perceived to be among the most nonreligious of the founding fathers; therefore his views serve the purposes of those who hope for a secular America. If this is so, it is a view rooted in ignorance both of Jefferson and the founding generation.

Yet, while Justice Black relied almost exclusively upon Jefferson's words to establish his interpretation of the First Amendment, he relied almost exclusively upon James Madison for his understanding of religion and the founding generation. This is as great an error as Black's misuse of Jefferson. Like Jefferson, Madison's views changed. Like Jefferson, Madison was but one of dozens of men whose views ought to have been considered by the *Everson* Court.

Still, Madison's views have a better claim for consideration than Jefferson's because he was actually involved in framing the First Amendment. Even here, Justice Black fails to do justice to history. In his writing for the majority, he never mentions Madison's proposed language for the First Amendment or what Madison's intent might have been. Instead, Black draws heavily upon Madison's "Memorial and Remonstrance" (see appendix 2), a document which must be understood against the broader fabric of Madison's life.

Madison's "Memorial" was an answer to a Virginia bill designed to provide government support for teachers of the Christian religion. Though fellow founders like Patrick Henry supported the measure, Madison was vehemently opposed and attacked the pending bill in fifteen individually numbered arguments, which comprised his "Memorial and Remonstrance." Madison's central concern was that if the state of Virginia could support the teaching of Christianity in general, the legislature could also subsidize one sect over all others.

Who does not see that the same authority which can establish Christianity, in exclusion of all of Religions, may establish with the same ease any particular sect of Christians, in exclusion of all other sects? That the same authority which can force a citizen to contribute

three pence only of his property for the support of any one establishment, may force him to conform to any other establishment in all
cases whatsoever?[9]

In similar fashion, Madison's fifteen points of the "Memorial"
raised heated opposition to state endorsement of an official religion,
and the bill was defeated.

The defeat of the Virginia "Bill establishing a provision for
Teachers of the Christian Religion" is often taken as a sign of the
mood of the country at the time. It was not. Similar bills were easily
passed in Massachusetts, New Hampshire, and Maryland, and even in
Virginia such national leaders as George Washington, John Marshall,
and Richard Henry Lee were in favor of the measure.

Still, the debate surrounding the Virginia bill does provide opportunity to know James Madison's views on matters of religion, as does
the "Detached Memorandum" he wrote many years after leaving
office. This "Memoranda" is a strange document, largely lost until
1946 when it was discovered among Madison's papers and published
in the *William and Mary Quarterly*—one year before the *Everson*
case. The document leaves no doubt that in his latter years Madison
firmly believed that the appointment of chaplains to the United
States Congress and presidential recommendations of national days
of thanksgiving and fasting were violations of the First Amendment.
Justice Black drew heavily upon these views in his *Everson* opinion, as
have those who see in Madison's words the expression of a secular
consensus among the founding fathers.

In fact, the "Memoranda" is not even sufficient to summarize
Madison's life and views, much less those of the founding generation. Madison, after all, sat on the very committee that appointed
congressional chaplains. Madison recommended days of thanksgiving
and fasting while he was president. These and other departures from

what seem on the surface to be unswerving ultra-separationist views bring into question Justice Black's use of Madison as a consistent example. Like Jefferson, Madison changed, contradicted himself, and deferred to the opinions of others. This, of course, is the problem with basing the understanding of an entire generation of founding fathers on two men. It is difficult enough to know one man's thinking over a lifetime given the shifting tides of the human mind. How much more difficult to attempt to summarize 126 founding fathers through the lives of two men. This is just what Justice Black attempted, and it is why he failed miserably.

Yet of all the failures and misreadings to be found in Justice Black's *Everson* ruling, it is the application of the First Amendment to the states that is, along with the misuse of Jefferson's phrase, the greatest folly. It is here that the greatest damage was done, here that the greatest violence to original intent was accomplished, and here that the clear counsel of history was most arrogantly ignored.

There is little question that the Bill of Rights was designed for two purposes: (1) to guarantee the people that the federal government would not encroach on their civil liberties and (2) to guarantee the states that the federal government would not tread upon their authority. This understanding of the Bill of Rights was even clarified in the landmark case *Barron v. Baltimore* of 1833, in which Chief Justice John Marshall spoke for a unified court in saying, "The Constitution was ordained and established by the people of the United States for themselves, for their own government and not for the government of the individual States." Therefore, the Bill of Rights "contains no expression indicating an intention to apply them to the state governments."[10] The Court rejected attempts to apply the Bill of Rights to the states on numerous occasions. Clearly, in early America, the Constitution was understood to fence in the federal government in order to protect and liberate the people and the states.

This understanding of federalism never came into question until after the Civil War with the passage of amendments designed to end slavery. The Thirteenth Amendment confirmed the abolition of slavery, and the Fifteenth Amendment made clear that the right to vote could not be denied "on account of race, color or previous condition of servitude."[11] It was the Fourteenth Amendment, though, that was not only the longest but by far the most controversial of the Amendments:

> All persons born or naturalized in the United States, and subject to the jurisdiction thereof, are citizens of the United States and of the State wherein they reside. No State shall make or enforce any law which shall abridge the privileges or immunities of citizens of the United States; nor shall any State deprive any person of life, liberty, or property, without due process of law; nor deny to any person within its jurisdiction the equal protection of the laws.[12]

The Amendment was designed to guarantee freed slaves their rights under the Constitution. Yet the wording raised a question: Did Congress intend the Fourteenth Amendment to apply the Bill of Rights to the states? It was something that had never been done before, and some suggested that this might be a result of the amendment. The Supreme Court made itself clear on the matter in cases like the famous *Slaughter-House Cases* of 1872 and *Hurtado v. California* of 1884. Emphatically and within sixteen years of the Fourteenth Amendment's ratification, the Court rejected all attempts to apply the Bill of Rights to the states.

The US Congress spoke clearly as well, particularly as regards religion and the states. In 1875, Representative James Blaine of Maine proposed legislation before Congress that would have made the First Amendment applicable to the states. The language of the resolution quoted the Establishment Clause nearly verbatim and made it—along with other provisions—binding on the states. Congress specifically rejected the resolution, and this is particularly significant given that the Congress that assembled in 1875 included twenty-three members of the Congress who had only seven years earlier adopted the Fourteenth Amendment. Clearly, these twenty-three members of Congress knew what was intended by the language of the Fourteenth Amendment, and it was obviously not to apply the First Amendment to the states. Years later, Judge William Brevard Hand concluded that the Blaine Amendment's defeat was "stark testimony to the fact the adopters of the Fourteenth Amendment never intended to incorporate the establishment clause of the First Amendment against the states."[13] Even more convincing is that between 1870 and 1950, the US Congress defeated the Blaine Amendment or similar proposals at least twenty-five times. Clearly, the US Congress had no intention of applying the Bill of Rights to the states through the Fourteenth Amendment.

Unfortunately, this did not stop the Supreme Court of the twentieth century. In 1925, the Court undermined the rulings of nearly a century and determined in *Gitlow v. People of the State of New York* that:

> For present purposes we may and do assume that freedom of speech and of the press—which are protected by the First Amendment from abridgement by Congress—are among the fundamental personal rights and "liberties" protected by the due process clause of the Fourteenth Amendment from impairment by the States.

This was a tragic departure from the intention of Congress and the wisdom of earlier court rulings. The door had been pried open, though. In 1931, in a case called *Near v. State of Minnesota ex rel. Olson*, the Court began restricting the states by using a piecemeal "incorporation" of amendments one through eight in the Bill of Rights. The vehicle for this was the Fourteenth Amendment, which the Court insisted was designed to apply the Bill of Rights to the states at least in some matters. The foundation had been laid. In *Cantwell v. Connecticut* of 1940 and then *Everson v. Board of Education* in 1947, the Court applied the first ten words of the Bill of Rights to the states in a manner that arrogantly rejected the counsel of history.

It is a difficult position to defend in light of that history. The founding generation fears an overreaching central government, particularly on matters of religion, and so it crafts an amendment—specifically addressed to that central government—which forbids it from making an official religion, thus leaving all matters of religion to the states. Years later, that amendment is applied as a restriction on the very states it was designed to protect. Now we have in America the odd practice of expecting the states to obey an amendment that is so specifically intended for Congress that it addresses Congress by name. Now, in the tangled reasoning of the Court, California must obey a statement in the Bill of Rights that says, "Congress shall make no law . . ."

That the *Everson* ruling was convoluted both because of its misuse of Jefferson's "wall of separation" metaphor and because of its wrongful application of the First Amendment to the states was recognized by later courts. Chief Justice Burger declared that "the line of separation, far from being a 'wall,' is a blurred, indistinct, and variable barrier depending on all the circumstances of a particular relationship."[14] Utah Supreme Court Justice Dallin Oakes, noting that the Court in *Everson* allowed buses to take children to religious schools but that other courts denied the legality of school prayer, wryly noted, "Certainly there is something anomalous about a wall that will admit a school bus without the 'slightest breach,' but is impermeable to a prayer . . . The metaphor is not an aid to thought and it can be a positive barrier to communication."[15]

The most devastating critique of the *Everson* case, though, came from then Supreme Court Justice and later Chief Justice William Rehnquist. His dissent in a case called *Wallace v. Jaffree*, an Alabama school prayer case decided in 1985, is often called "The Anti-*Everson*" and is a brilliant dissection of Justice Hugo Black's flawed recounting of history and weak legal reasoning (see appendix 2).

Opening with the assertion that "it is impossible to build sound constitutional doctrine upon a mistaken understanding of constitutional history," Rehnquist complained that the "Establishment Clause has been freighted with Jefferson's misleading metaphor for nearly 40 years." He followed with page after page of carefully recounted history: of the constitutional debates, of the writings of Madison and Jefferson, of the acts of the early federal government. His conclusion was that in early America the first ten words of the Bill of Rights simply "forbade establishment of a national religion and forbade preference among religious sects or denominations." Nothing more.

Having defined the meaning of the Establishment Clause, Judge Rehnquist then criticized the Court's rulings since *Everson* with a frankness rare even in dissenting opinions:

> Notwithstanding the absence of a historical basis for this theory of rigid separation, the wall idea might well have served as a useful albeit misguided analytical concept, had it led this Court to unified and principled results in Establishment Clause cases. The opposite, unfortunately, has been true; in the 38 years since *Everson* our Establishment Clause cases have been neither principled nor unified. Our recent opinions, many of them hopelessly divided pluralities, have with embarrassing candor conceded that the "wall of separation" is merely a "blurred, indistinct, and variable barrier," which "is not wholly accurate" and can only be "dimly perceived."

These were shockingly harsh words, but Justice Rehnquist had yet to finish. He understood better than most the damage done by the Court's foolish misapplication of history and law, and he hoped to bring this folly to an end.

> Whether due to its lack of historical support or its practical unwork-ablity, the *Everson* "wall" has proved all but useless as a guide to sound constitutional adjudication. It illustrates only too well the wisdom of Benjamin Cardozo's observation that "[m]etaphors in law are to be narrowly watched, for starting as devices to liberate thought, they end often by enslaving it."
>
> But the greatest injury of the "wall" notion is its mischievous diversion of judges from the actual intentions of the drafters of the Bill of Rights. The "crucible of litigation," is well adapted to adjudicating factual disputes on the basis of testimony presented in court, but no amount of repetition of historical errors in judicial opinions can make the errors true. The "wall of separation between church and State" is a metaphor based on bad history, a metaphor which has proved useless as a guide to judging. It should be frankly and explicitly abandoned.[16]

Judge Rehnquist was typically brilliant, prophetic, and unheeded. Sadly, what he described as a "misguided metaphor" has not been abandoned, and the *Everson* misapplication of law and history haunts the nation to this day. Consider the following rulings by the US Supreme Court or other courts that have built upon the foundation laid by Justice Black in the *Everson* case:

- A verbal prayer offered in a school is unconstitutional, even if it is both denominationally neutral and voluntarily participated in. *Engel v. Vitale*, 1962; *Abington v. Schempp*, 1963; *Commissioner of Education v. School Committee of Leyden*, 1971.

- Freedom of speech is guaranteed to students who speak at school assemblies where attendance is voluntary unless that speech includes a prayer. *Stein v. Oshinsky*, 1965; *Collins v. Chandler Unified School District*, 1981.

- If a student prays over lunch, it is unconstitutional for him to pray aloud. *Reed v. van Hoven*, 1965.

- It is unconstitutional for kindergarten students to recite: "We thank you for the birds that sing; We thank you [God] for everything," even though the word "God" is not uttered. *DeSpain v. DeKalb County Community School District*, 1967.

- It is unconstitutional to set up a nativity scene in the lobby of a county government building. *County of Allegheny v. American Civil Liberties Union Greater Pittsburgh Chapter*, 1989.

- It is unconstitutional for a war memorial to be erected in the shape of a cross. *Lowe v. City of Eugene*, 1969.

- It is unconstitutional for students to arrive at school early to hear a student volunteer read prayers. *State Board of Education v. Board of Education of Netcong*, 1970.

- It is unconstitutional for a Board of Education to "reference" God or "Biblical instruction" in any of its official writings related to standards for operation of schools. *State v. Whisner*, 1976.

- It is unconstitutional for a classroom library to contain books that deal with Christianity or for a teacher to be seen with a personal copy of the Bible at school. *Roberts v. Madigan*, 1990.

- It is unconstitutional for a public cemetery to have a planter in the shape of a cross because it might cause "emotional distress" and constitute an "injury-in-fact." *Warsaw v. Tehachapi*, 1990.

- It is unconstitutional for the Ten Commandments to hang on the walls of a classroom even if they are purchased by private funds. *Stone v. Graham*, 1980; *Ring v. Grand Forks Public School District*, 1980; *Lanner v. Wimmer*, 1981.

- A bill becomes unconstitutional even though the wording may be constitutionally acceptable, if the legislator who introduced the bill had a religious purpose in his mind when he authored it. *Wallace v. Jaffree*, 1985.

- It is unconstitutional for a kindergarten class to recite: "God is great, God is good, let us thank Him for our food." *Wallace v. Jaffree*, 1984.

- It is unconstitutional for a graduation ceremony to contain an opening or a closing prayer. *Graham v. Central Community School District*, 1985; *Disselbrett v. Douglas School District*, 1986.

- In a city seal, it is unconstitutional for any symbol to depict religious heritage or any religious element of the community. *Robinson v. City of Edmond*, 1995; *Harris v. City of Zion*, 1991; *Kuhn v. City of Rolling Meadows*, 1991; *Friedman v. Board of County Commissioners*, 1985.

- It is unconstitutional for a kindergarten class to ask during a school assembly whose birthday is celebrated on Christmas. *Florey v. Sioux Falls School District*, 1979.

Clearly, post-*Everson* "search and destroy" efforts against public expressions of faith are dismantling a valuable heritage. In 1979, for example, two Harvard law students—some said merely to impress their constitutional law professor—filed a lawsuit to challenge the constitutionality of the American military chaplaincy. As doubtful as the effort sounds, it almost succeeded. Had the case not dragged on for seven years and had the students not run out of money, *Katcoff v. Marsh* may well have become infamous as the case that ended the two-hundred-year-old, vital work of military chaplains.[17] This is the legacy of *Everson*.

Then there are the absurdities that reveal how unwise and unworkable the *Everson* ruling was. In Pennsylvania, because a prosecuting attorney mentioned seven words from the Bible in the courtroom, a jury sentence was overturned for a man convicted of brutally clubbing a seventy-one-year-old woman to death.[18] Though states print hundreds of thousands of custom license plates, Oregon refused to print "Pray," Virginia refused to print "God 4 Us," and Utah refused to print "Thank God," claiming that such wording violated "the separation of church and state."[19] And a federal judge forbade a high-ranking official from the national drug czar's office, known to be an expert in his field, from giving a secular antidrug message in a public school because the expert was also an ordained Christian minister.[20] Such miscarriages of justice are the product of a legal system more focused upon a mythical wall of separation between church and state than it is upon simple justice.

What is certain is that Chief Justice Rehnquist was right: the *Everson* case applied a murky metaphor in a manner that has inspired unprincipled, misguided, and embarrassing rulings. Perhaps more, at a time when a widespread resurgence of faith is offering fresh energy and wisdom to American culture, the *Everson* case and its judicial children are placing increasing power into the hands of a secularist elite that threatens to complete the demolition of the nation's religious heritage and the theft of the people's religious rights. It is just this battle between the legacy of *Everson* and the renewed spirituality of the American people that is creating one of the great cultural dramas of our time, as we shall see.

77

4

FAITH-BASED BLACKMAIL

It is hard to know what inspires him most when he remembers his friend, Cesar Chavez. To be sure, the images are seldom far from his mind—memories of Cesar sounding the trumpet for farm workers' rights or of Cesar enduring the rage of a comfortable nation in the 1960s and 1970s. But which memory of his heroic friend stirs him most today?

Perhaps it is knowing that Cesar had gone to work in the fields at an early age and never finished the eighth grade, but his office walls were lined with books of philosophy and economics, with studies of Gandhi and Lincoln. Perhaps it was what Cesar had seen: the navy for two years and that after a life of dirt floor shacks and near starvation wages. But then it may have simply been Cesar's poetic soul. He said things like, "The love for justice that is in us is not only the best part of our being; it is also the most true to our nature."

It is hard to know. Whatever it is, Rees Lloyd believes that Cesar Chavez was "in his humility and sacrifice, the greatest man I ever knew, or will know, and I will always walk in his shadow."

This is saying a great deal, for Rees has known some heroes in his time. He worked with Martin Luther King Jr. in the Poor People's Campaign of 1968, fought for civil rights at the side of Chicano advocate Reies Lopez Tijerina, and marched with some of the leading voices for change in recent American history.

Yet Rees's life on the cutting edge of social reform is not what first springs to mind to see him today. He is somewhat of a contradiction. He peers out at the world through laughing Welsh eyes but speaks in a manner that pleasantly recalls his early years as an Indiana steel worker and trucker. He wears blue jeans with bolo ties and carries saddle bags instead of a briefcase while his associates don business suits, yet the men in those suits gladly yield to his rapid-fire intelligence and passion. Those who know him only by reputation probably expect an old hippy activist hanging on to sweet memories of battles passed, but Rees Lloyd spends most of his time talking about how the present is fashioning the future.

Perhaps this is what Cesar saw—these contradictions, this ability to straddle cultures—that moved him to tell Rees Lloyd one day that he should go to law school. Rees agreed, and soon found that law was something he did well. Very well. In fact, while in school Rees received a fellowship from the American Civil Liberties Union, and after graduation in 1979, he joined the ACLU as a staff attorney. This is when he began to soar.

He did work on employment rights cases that he is still proud of and even helped found the ACLU Workers Rights Committee. His reputation grew. His untiring mind and devotion to justice made him a formidable force for good. The ACLU commended him for "pioneering efforts in the area of workers rights," and he was honored by the California State Assembly and Senate as well as a dozen civil rights-oriented organizations. Rees Lloyd became the lawyer Cesar Chavez always knew he could be. In fact, the greatest commendation he ever received was when Cesar told the *Los Angeles Times* that Rees was "an attorney, but he's really an advocate for human rights. He's very committed and not too worried about money." Rees would treasure these words all his life.

In time, he would move on from the ACLU, serving workers unions, Cesar's United Farm Worker's organization, and a host of causes that benefited from his vision and skill. Today, in what seems to some like a strange departure from the early path of his life, Rees serves the American Legion, the intensely patriotic organization begun after

World War I in service of "God and Country," the words which form their motto. And Rees is in his element. As a veteran, a patriot, and a lover of democracy, he has found both his tribe and his cause.

There is something that troubles him, though. It has to do with the ACLU he once respected and served so well. Though during his years there the ACLU never filed a suit regarding religion as far as he remembers, filing Establishment Clause suits seems to be almost all they do now.

And it is more than troubling, more than embarrassing. It is alarming. The same organization that once valiantly championed the rights of the oppressed now devotes itself to irrelevant religious nitpicking. How silly that the ACLU would spend so much time and money opposing the seal of the county of Los Angeles because it had a tiny cross on it commemorating the region's Spanish mission heritage!

Then there was the case that landed closer to home. To honor World War I veterans, private citizens in Arizona fashioned two pieces of metal into a cross and mounted it on a rock outcrop eleven miles from the nearest highway. That was in 1934. Everything was fine until President Clinton incorporated the site into the Mohave National Preserve. Then the ACLU saw its opportunity and filed a suit to have the cross removed as a violation of the Constitution.

Even this didn't surprise Rees. He had seen it before. What shocked him was how the ACLU was profiting from the suit. Since the laws allow plaintiffs who win civil rights cases to have their legal fees paid, the ACLU was making tens of thousands of dollars for doing nothing more than destroying a symbol of faith and a statement of honor for America's heroes.

It was a travesty and of the kind Rees Lloyd knew well. In fact, he had spent his whole career fighting oppression and injustice, and he wasn't willing to sit silently by while the ACLU blanketed the country with its own form of religious bigotry.

That's when Rees Lloyd and the American Legion went on the move. Now they are on the forefront of the battle to preserve the rights of Americans. And Rees Lloyd is taking no prisoners. Calling the ACLU "the Taliban of American liberal secularism," he is fighting like the champion of rights that he is. He has met this enemy before, after all: in migrant worker camps, in poverty-ridden tenements, in oppressive factories and shops. It is the suffocating wickedness of legalized tyranny, and Rees Lloyd plans to bring it to an end.

Cesar would expect no less.

WHEN THE UNITED STATES SUPREME COURT ISSUED ITS RULING IN *Everson v. Board of Education*—determining that the Constitution permits no government connection to religion in any form—it quickly became obvious that a gap existed between the law and the practice of a century and a half. How was this gap to be closed? How was Justice Black's extreme separation of church and state to be accomplished? There are no official religious police in America, and the law enforcement that existed at the time frankly had better things to do than strip religious symbols from government buildings or stand guard over schoolchildren tempted to pray.

The answer appeared almost immediately after the Court's ruling. The enforcement would come from private organizations determined to search out and destroy, through litigation, any connection between government and religion. These groups became, in effect, *Everson*'s private army, and their impact on the role of religion in America would prove transforming.

Yet these unofficial religious police were successful primarily because they were armed by courts and politicians in ways often unintended and frequently unjust. It is a tale that begs to be told, one of the defining sagas of our time, and it is best begun several decades after the *Everson* ruling, when religious cultures were clashing in the wake of a troubled decade.

It is not difficult now, from the distance of years, to understand the questioning and self-doubt that filled the United States in the mid-1970s. Americans had just emerged from the upheavals of the 1960s only to be confronted in the early years of the next decade with the Watergate scandal, the resignation of a president, an economic depression, and what appeared to be a dishonorable end to the Vietnam War. All of this occurred as the nation's bicentennial approached, which raised its own disturbing questions about what America had become. It was, understandably, a season of disillusionment, and it gave birth in turn to a season of spiritual longing.

Religion, then, moved center stage. For many Americans, this began when Georgia governor and presidential candidate Jimmy Carter started speaking openly about being "born again." Observers quickly understood that Carter was giving voice to what a quiet multitude believed, a wide swath of middle class, middle-aged, middle Americans who clung tenaciously to their traditional faith, rejected the radicalism of the 1960s, grieved the despair of the nation in its two hundredth year, and yearned for a return to a better day. It was to awaken this sleeping giant that new voices began to be heard, voices that signaled what has come to be known as the rise of the Religious Right.

These voices belonged to men like Jerry Falwell, Pat Robertson, D. James Kennedy, and James Robison—men who believed that legal and cultural trends were tearing the nation away from her religious moorings, that there had been an earlier, more righteous era in American history to which the modern generation ought to return. Their opinions were nothing new, of course, but their methods were. They mobilized the religion of the pew to make it the religion of the ballot box and accomplished this on the strength of innovative organizations and media presence of a kind previously unknown in

American religion. By the end of the decade, Jerry Falwell would head an organization of millions called the Moral Majority, Pat Robertson would lay the foundation for a media ministry of international scope, and both Kennedy and Robison would speak to millions and mentor some of the most powerful politicians in the country. All of these men urged a vital truth upon their followers: religion ought to influence political behavior.

This belief, a comfort to millions, terrified millions more, among them a successful writer and television producer named Norman Lear. Most Americans in the 1970s knew his name. If not, they certainly knew his work, for he was the guiding spirit behind some of the most popular and controversial television shows in the nation's history. Among them were *All in the Family*; *Good Times*; *Sanford and Son*; *Mary Hartman, Mary Hartman*; *The Jeffersons*; and *One Day at a Time*, to name but a few. At a time when the wasteland of television was populated by shows like *Green Acres* and *The Beverly Hillbillies*, Lear's productions were bright and innovative commentaries on American life. Audiences watched them, discussed them, and were changed.

What most Americans did not know, however, was that from 1971 to 1979 Norman Lear was the president of the American Civil Liberties Union in Southern California. Those familiar with the ACLU would not have been surprised. The truth is that Lear's work and vision were very much in keeping with the work and vision of the ACLU's founder, Roger Baldwin.

Born in 1884 to descendants of the Pilgrim fathers, Baldwin was raised in an upper-class Boston family that was prosperous, well-educated, progressive, and civic minded. It was also troubled—rent by strife, adultery, and divorce. Baldwin turned for solace to his anti-Christian grandfather, William Henry Baldwin, and found in him what he would later call "the moving force" behind his "liberal" and "nonconformist" upbringing.[1] Immersed in a world of radical reform from an early age, young Roger followed his grandfather into a life-long moralistic rebellion against the church and followed a favorite aunt into a lifelong association with anticapitalistic fringe groups. He later entered Harvard, he said, because it was "a place where dissent in any form was quite respectable."[2]

After graduation and the grand tour of Europe expected of Boston's wealthy young men, Baldwin threw himself into a series of radical causes. He moved to St. Louis to teach sociology at Washington University. There he helped organize the St. Louis City Club, a luncheon gathering for political discussion, and invited prominent suffragettes, Socialists, anarchists, and Communists to speak. He also attended meetings of the International Workers of the World—a Marxism-tinged labor organization—and served in local politics, working to reorganize the municipal government of St. Louis.

Still, he was unsatisfied and feared he might descend into "Salon Socialism" or "Arm Chair Bolshevism." His chance to prove himself came in 1917 when he was invited to work for the American Union Against Militarism (AUAM), a pacifist lobbying group opposed to United States involvement in the First World War. He left St. Louis for his new assignment on April 2. On April 6, the United States officially joined the Allies in the "war to end all wars." By May 18, Congress had approved the Selective Service Act. Baldwin was aghast and determined to fight his government's involvement in the war. On May 19, one day after Congress instituted the draft, he founded the Bureau of Conscientious Objectors, which was designed to serve the needs and defend the cause of draft dodgers. The Bureau became the most active and visible branch of the AUAM.

The new organization met with a firestorm of opposition. The *New York Times* criticized it by saying that Baldwin and his associates were "antagonizing the settled policies of the government, resisting the execution of its deliberately formed plans, and gaining for themselves immunity from the application of laws to which all other good citizens willingly submit."[3] To quell the fears of the AUAM board and assuage widespread animosity, Baldwin renamed the organization the Civil Liberties Bureau. It didn't help. Matters grew worse, and finally the AUAM board voted to sever all ties with Baldwin and his Bureau. He was unbowed, renaming his organization the National Civil Liberties Bureau.

Baldwin seemed only emboldened by the controversies that surrounded him. One of the first pieces of literature he wrote for the new Bureau was declared "unmailable" by the Post Office because of its "radical and subversive views." Then his offices were raided by the FBI, and his files were confiscated. Twelve days later, he was called to register for the draft. He had been waiting for the chance to resist, though, and proclaimed at his trial that he was a committed anarchist, that he was associated with the International Workers of the World, and that he was pledged to Socialist reform. He was sentenced to a year in a penitentiary.

Following prison, he married a woman named Madeline Doty, whom he abandoned two months later. He then determined to authenticate his socialism by laboring among the proletariat. He shoveled iron ore at a steel mill, loaded raw materials in a brickyard, and labored on a railroad construction crew. After three months, he abandoned this too, confiding later, "I'd rather be the friend of the workingman than be the workingman: it's a lot easier."[4]

Realizing his life's calling, he returned to his Civil Liberties Bureau and worked to give it new life. Renaming it the American Civil Liberties Union, he then moved it into New York offices, which it shared with a Communist Party publication. This proximity drew him into sympathy for the Soviet cause. He would eventually conclude that the Soviet regime was "the greatest and most daring experiment yet undertaken to recreate society in terms of human values."[5] Opponents quipped that Baldwin had 20/20 vision in his right eye but was blind in his left, meaning he could see the problems with the capitalist West but could see nothing wrong with Socialist Russia. In his *Liberty Under the Soviets*, written after a happy visit to Russia, Baldwin admitted that the Soviet government had instituted "complete censorship of all means of communications and the complete suppression of any organized opposition to the dictatorship or its program."[6] He went on to state that "no civil liberty as we understand it in the West exists for the opponents of the regime."[7] Nevertheless, he celebrated the Soviet State for the "far more significant freedom of workers," the "abolition of the privileged classes," the "revolution in education," and the "liberty won for anti-religion."[8]

Critics wondered how a man supposedly devoted to civil liberties in the United States could excuse civil rights abuses in Russia. Baldwin explained that "repressions in Western Democracies are violations of professed constitutional liberties, and I condemn them as such. Repressions in Soviet Russia are the weapons of struggle in a transition period to Socialism."[9] This explanation didn't help, nor did Baldwin's assertion that "when the power of the working class is once achieved, as it has been only in the Soviet Union, I am for maintaining it by any means whatever." Nor was Baldwin well served when he proclaimed, "No champion of a Socialist society could fail to see that some suppression was necessary to achieve it."[10]

Failing to reconcile these polarities in his thinking, Baldwin finally joined scores of "United Front" organizations that were barely concealed recruiting centers for the Communist Party. Years later he explained, "I joined. I don't regret being a part of the Communist tactic which increased the effectiveness of a good cause. I knew what I was doing. I was not an innocent liberal. I wanted what the Communists wanted and I traveled the United Front road to get it."[11] The work of the American Civil Liberties Union at the time reflected Baldwin's devotion to communism. A congressional investigation in the early 1930s concluded that of the ACLU Board and National Committee members elected during the first sixty years of the organization's history, almost 80 percent had Communist affiliations.[12] The ACLU was soon labeled a "Communist Front" organization. Even the labor unions the ACLU had first arisen to support distanced themselves.[13]

Baldwin remained defiant in his support of communism throughout the 1930s. As he wrote a friend, "I see so much to be said for the destruction of privilege based on wealth that I will stand for Russia against the rest of the world."[14] Then the unexpected happened. On August 20, 1939, Baldwin's hero, Joseph Stalin, signed a nonaggression pact with a man Baldwin hated and whom he regarded as the perfect opposite to all he held dear: Adolf Hitler. Baldwin was deflated, but more importantly his eyes were opened, finally, to Soviet intentions.

Comedian Dick Gregory has said, "Hell hath no fury like a liberal scorned."[15] In just such a fury, Baldwin distanced himself and the ACLU from the Communist Party and redirected the organization's focus away from international politics and onto reform through the courts. As he wrote to his Communist friend, Louis Lochner, "We want to look like patriots in everything we do. We want to get a lot of flags, talk a great deal about the Constitution and what our forefathers wanted to make of this country and to show that we are the fellows that really stand for the spirit of our institutions."[16] The tactic worked. By the end of the Second World War, the ACLU had been accepted into the mainstream. One of its members—Felix Frankfurter—had been elevated to the Supreme Court, another—Francis Biddle—had become US attorney general. Succeeding presidential administrations would be filled with high-level ACLU members. If this wasn't sufficient evidence of mainstream status, it would arrive with certainty in 1981 when President Jimmy Carter, in one of his final acts in office, awarded Roger Baldwin the Medal of Freedom—the nation's highest civilian honor.

This was odd tribute for an unapologetic Communist. Still, Baldwin's communism does explain his views on one aspect of the ACLU's work: religion. The Soviet Constitution of 1947 had stated, "In order to ensure to citizens freedom of conscience, the church in the USSR is separated from the state, and the school from the church. Freedom of religious worship and freedom of anti-religious propaganda is recognized for all citizens."[17] This promise of freedom of worship would be proven false by Soviet history, but the supposed devotion to a separation of church and state would attract secularists like Baldwin who wished the same for the United States. The ACLU reflected Baldwin's dream of a secular America and sought to achieve it under a banner of separation of church and state.

Even before the *Everson* case confused the Establishment Clause with seven words from Thomas Jefferson's Danbury letter, the ACLU sought out opportunities to contest religion in American public life. In 1925, the ACLU printed an advertisement offering its services to anyone willing to challenge a Tennessee law that forbade the teaching of evolution. A biology teacher in Dayton named John T. Scopes volunteered. What resulted was one of the most famous trials in American history. Called the Scopes Monkey Trial, the great contest pitted former vice president William Jennings Bryan against the famous agnostic lawyer Clarence Darrow in a clash of faiths that captured the attention of the nation.[18] Though Scopes was ultimately found guilty and fined one hundred dollars, the trial stirred just the kind of antireligion media storm the ACLU had hoped for and signaled an early stepping onto the religious battlefield for Baldwin's young organization. There were many more such battles to come.

This brings us back to Norman Lear as the president of the ACLU of Southern California in the mid-1970s. While his avant garde situation comedies skillfully jabbed at traditional American ideals, Lear worried about the rise of the Religious Right and its attempt to bring religion to bear upon public policy. He feared that men like Falwell and Robertson intended to erect an American theocracy that would trample what he understood to be the constitutional separation of church and state. The soul of the nation was in the balance, he believed, and he had to act.

According to former ACLU attorney Rees Lloyd, in the late 1970s, just as Falwell's Moral Majority began marshalling strength, Lear approached the ACLU about more aggressively pursuing Establishment Clause cases in the courts. Such suits had been part of the ACLU's work but not its primary focus. Lear believed the time had come for a concentrated counterassault on the Religious Right and urged the ACLU to dedicate an entire division to the cause. In return, Lear offered funding and teamed with his friend and fellow activist Stanley Sheinbaum to begin channeling "Hollywood money" into the ACLU's coffers. The sums were huge and not only enabled the organization to fight any intrusion of religion into the public sphere that it deemed an infringement of the Constitution but also to hire Sheinbaum's assistant, Carol Sobel, as the ACLU of Southern California's first Establishment Clause attorney. A permanent shift in focus had occurred in the ACLU, powered largely by money and Norman Lear's personal influence.[19]

Still concerned about the influence of televangelists on American politics, Lear continued searching for more effective ways to shape public opinion. He decided to lean to his own strengths, and in 1980 he started an organization called People for the American Way, along with luminaries like Congresswoman Barbara Jordan and Notre Dame's Father Theodore Hesburgh. Lear launched his new organization by producing a series of television commercials and prime-time specials designed to counter the message of the Religious Right.

These broadcasts drew widespread attention in large part because they starred celebrities like Muhammad Ali and Goldie Hawn. As Lear later explained:

> I didn't start out by trying to found an organization at all. I saw Falwell, Robertson, Swaggart, and all those fellows, and I thought they were abusing religion. Most people I knew laughed them off, but I got an idea to do a motion picture called *Religion*, and I started to watch all these shows eight, ten hours a week. It was sobering. And I started to say, "This is not my America. You don't mix politics and religion this way." They railed against the Supreme Court, the public school system, secular humanism—often with thinly veiled anti-Semitic and anti-Catholic intolerance. You don't wish Supreme Court justices dead with a Bible in your hand as Swaggart once did. They exploited their followers' needs for their own ends, and insisted that federal law ought to embody sectarian beliefs.
>
> My goal was simply to get another message on the tube. So I went out at my own expense and made three or four thirty-second commercials. I had a working stiff like Archie Bunker. I always try to think what the average guy is thinking. In them, he says that a bunch of preachers came on TV trying to tell him what to think on political issues—that he and his family are good Christians or bad Christians depending on their political point of view. He knows there's got to be something wrong when somebody tells you you're a good Christian or a bad Christian depending on your political views.[20]

Lear's productions were effective and won widespread support for People for the American Way. Over the following decades, the organization branched out from its media focus to counter what it deemed to be academic censorship, a lack of textbooks teaching evolution, the Supreme Court nomination of Robert Bork, a constitutional amendment prohibiting flag burning, attacks on the National Endowment of the Humanities, the use of the Bible as a textbook, prayer in public schools, and the influence of the "Radical Right" in the American judiciary.

As opposition to the rise of the Religious Right gathered momentum, new organizations joined the fray. Among the most effective was Americans United for Separation of Church and State (AUSCS). Founded in 1947 to oppose government aid to religious schools, the organization stepped onto the forefront of Establishment Clause issues when Barry Lynn became its executive director in 1992. Prior to that appointment, Lynn had served as the legislative counsel for the Washington office of the American Civil Liberties Union from 1984 to 1991.

Lynn quickly became the most visible face of the ultra-separationist view of church and state. Today, a decade and a half after assuming his role, he seems almost ever-present when Establishment Clause issues fill the headlines and presses his case with a rigorous consistency that often cows his opponents. His effectiveness is due in part to his credentials. He is both an ordained United Church of Christ minister and a lawyer with a degree from Georgetown. This background removes the antireligion stigma that is sometimes attached to leaders of other organizations and gives Lynn a hearing in communities of faith that he would not otherwise have.

The Americans United for Separation of Church and State are effective largely because of their mastery of a two-pronged approach. They educate and litigate with skill. While Barry Lynn dissects opponents on FOX or CNN, AUSCS's lawyers file strategic suits that capture the imaginations of donors. Coupled with these efforts are aggressive educational strategies that press an *Everson*-oriented understanding of American history into the popular mind. By staying focused on their message and marrying the courtroom to the newsroom, Barry Lynn and Americans United for Separation of Church and State have become a cultural force of exceptional influence.

A smaller but equally effective organization is the Freedom From Religion Foundation (FFRF). Founded by a feminist businesswoman from Wisconsin and three others, the organization is now the nation's largest association of atheists and agnostics and has won numerous legal challenges to the Bush administration's "faith-based initiatives." Unlike Barry Lynn, who endorses the private practice of religion but opposes any government support, the Freedom From Religion Foundation fights Establishment Clause cases in the courtroom as its way of fighting religion in general.

Its tactics are wisely chosen. Many of FFRF's personnel were once clergy or among the deeply religious and later experienced "deconversion." Understanding the natural doubts of the religious, FFRF plays to them. Their Web site offers an online quiz designed to make even experienced Bible students doubt their beliefs. Books and radio shows encourage supporters to envision a world without religion, and this same dream inspires legal challenges to most any joining of faith and government. The organization exercises a rigorous, almost lighthearted, consistency. Challenging a cross on public property in San Diego, the Freedom From Religion Foundation offered a monument dedicated to "Atheists in Foxholes" instead. Though the FFRF is smaller, angrier, more radical, and much broader in its purpose than other such organizations, its merging of the religiously disaffected with those eager to enforce a wide separation between church and state has made it one of the most effective organizations of its kind.

These then are the private organizations that have become the enforcers of the *Everson* vision. It is they who search out the entanglements between church and state, they who press the *Everson* legacy in the courts of the land, and they who stand guard on Jefferson's wall believing it to be a wall constructed by the US Constitution. They are wrong, of course, but they are sincere, effective, and, perhaps more important, they are currently winning.

Yet they are also not the crux of the story. True, they battle for a destruction of rights and heritage that the founding fathers sought to preserve. They are without question the stinging blade of secularism in our time, and they warrant opposition by those who know both the hopes of the founders and the value of faith to the Republic. Still, organizations like these will exist, and perhaps should. The religious should welcome them to the free market of ideas and be grateful for the sharpening of the sword of faith they effect through their opposition.

The problem is not that they exist. The problem is that they are preferred. They receive an empowering by law that ought not belong to any private organization, much less to those devoted to the destruction of the nation's heritage. Here is the offense: not that these organizations argue what they do in court, but rather that they do not fight on a level field of play, for the truth is that the law is weighted in favor of secularism.

This is a serious charge and demands explanation. Consider, then, the matter of what lawyers call "fee shifting." Throughout US history, an arrangement called the "American rule" usually governed the payment of attorneys' fees. Each side in a lawsuit, according to this rule, was responsible for its own legal fees regardless of the outcome of the case. Seldom would an American court ever require a participant in a lawsuit to pay his opponent's legal bills.

This began to change with the Civil Rights Act of 1964. Designed to end discrimination in a variety of forms based on race, color, sex, religion, or national origin, the act was a heroic advance in the battle for fulfillment of the American dream. There was a weakness in the act's provisions, though. Congress could guarantee civil rights as a matter of law all it wished, but assuring civil rights in practice called for courageous souls willing to file lawsuits against discrimination. This also called for money, though—something the lower-income individuals who were most likely to suffer discrimination did not have.

Realizing this check on the spirit of the Civil Rights Act, the courts began awarding legal fees to individuals who proved civil rights discrimination in court. In *Newman v. Piggie Park Enterprises* of 1968, for example, the court ruled that "one who succeeds in obtaining an injunction under Title II of the Civil Rights Acts of 1964 should ordinarily recover an attorney's fee."[21] The intention of such awards was not simply to reward courageous action against discrimination but to pay the fees of those whom the law called "private attorney generals," meaning those who brought lawsuits in pursuit of a public good. If a man suffering employment discrimination based on his skin color in Kansas successfully won his suit, the courts understood that this man had served the public in the same way that the attorney general of Kansas might: by filing a lawsuit to protect the people and assure justice. It would be legitimate, then, for the man to have his attorney's fees paid by those who had discriminated against him.

In 1975, the Supreme Court forced Congress to be more specific about the practice of fee shifting. In a case called *Alyeska Pipeline Service Co. v. Wilderness Society*, the Court ruled that it had no authority to require the payment of an opponent's legal fees without specific legislation governing the matter.[22] This stirred Congress to pass the Civil Rights Attorney's Fees Awards Act of 1976, which created a specific exception to the "American Rule" and defined how attorney's fees could be "shifted" under the provisions of the 1964 Civil Rights Act. The intent of the law was clear: to make sure that the underprivileged could secure their rights in court without having to wait for the cumbersome machinery of government and without having to pay devastating legal fees to obtain those rights.

The law was a noble attempt to protect the civil rights of those most vulnerable to abuse and least able to defend themselves. Sadly, though, the Civil Rights Attorney's Fees Awards Act, also known as 42 U.S.C., §1988, has become a cynical tool of destruction in the hands of the ACLU and its sister organizations. Requesting the benefits of "fee shifting" originally intended for the underprivileged, the ACLU now routinely enjoys having its legal fees paid by taxpayers when it wins a suit to safeguard its version of the Establishment Clause. This means that when such organizations file suit to remove a cross from public land or end a moment of silence at a public school, for example, public funds not only pay for a defense against the assault on religious liberties, but they also pay the bills for the assault if they lose in court.

The truth is that *Everson*'s private army receives staggering fees at public expense in return for destroying the nation's religious heritage and rights.

- When the ACLU, the Americans United for Separation of Church and State, and the Southern Poverty Law Center filed suit to remove the Ten Commandments from a display inside the Alabama State Judicial Building, the three organizations received attorney's fees in excess of $1.2 million.

- For driving the Boy Scouts of America's summer camp from San Diego's Balboa Park—where the event had been held since 1915—the ACLU received $790,000 in fees from taxpayers.

- The state of Kentucky paid the ACLU more than $121,500 in attorney fees after it lost a case regarding a Ten Commandments display outside of its capitol in Frankfort. This was on top of more than $700,000 the state paid from 1994 to 2003 in other cases pertaining to both abortion and religion.

- The Dover, Pennsylvania, School Board paid the ACLU, the Americans United for Separation of Church and State, and a private law firm more than $1.2 million when it lost the right to teach intelligent design as well as evolution in its curriculum.

- Perhaps oddest of all, the case of the cross in the Mohave Desert that so incensed Rees Lloyd and the American Legion is not even resolved yet as of this writing, but the ACLU has collected some $63,000 in fees.

Such fees have an intimidation factor all their own. When the ACLU threatened a suit to challenge the forty-seven-year-old seal of the County of Los Angeles because it had a tiny cross on it, the County changed the seal without a fight. It was willing to pay its own legal fees but could not afford to pay the ACLU's fees if it lost the suit. This story has been repeated often around the country. A school district bans before-school, voluntary student prayer meetings after one phone call from the ACLU. A state removes a religious symbol from a hundred-year-old monument after a single atheist merely threatens a call to Barry Lynn. Financially strapped school districts and local governments simply cannot endure the penalties the courts impose for fighting to preserve religious rights.

Equally troubling is that the awards made to ACLU-type organizations frequently do not reimburse real expenses. As former ACLU attorney Rees Lloyd explains, "The fact is that most of the ACLU's legal work is done either free, as *pro bono* work by big law firms, or is done by staff attorneys. Either way, there are little to no legal fees to pay no matter the size of the case and yet the courts allow the ACLU to compute fees based on the huge hourly rates of major law firms, some three to six hundred dollars an hour. This is pure profit for the ACLU, and this is also why they defend fee shifting so vigorously."[23]

This profit motive in fee shifting does not seem to bother some judges. In a case entitled *McLean v. Arkansas Board of Education*, which the Eighth Circuit Court of Appeals heard in 1983, the court ruled that the ACLU was due its legal fees in the case even though all of its costs were reimbursed through a fund-raising campaign.[24] The court ordered the defendants to pay all the ACLU's legal fees despite the fact that those fees had already been paid. This means that the ACLU's fees were paid twice, a huge profit for the organization, particularly given that the fees it requested were probably far beyond the amount actually spent on the case.

The noble intent of fee shifting has been lost through its use in Establishment Clause cases. This is not only because taxpayers are forced to pay for the destruction of their own rights, but also because they are sometimes kept from asserting their rights in court at all through intimidation. Suppose the grounds of a federal cemetery include a statue with a Star of David on it. The ACLU or another such organization files suit to have the symbol removed. A Jewish woman whose husband is buried in the cemetery may wish to join the defense of the symbol, but her lawyer would have to discourage it knowing that the woman would be exposed to massive fees if the case were lost. Thus, the very rights of the individual that fee shifting was designed to protect are trampled underfoot by the use of fee shifting in Establishment Clause cases.

Again, the laws are weighted in favor of secularism. The courts put weapons in the hands of *Everson*'s army that are unavailable to defenders of the founding generation's intentions for religion and government.

Another such weapon is found in the political restrictions placed on religious organizations in America. This is a practice with an unusual history but one that explains how easily religion is gagged in a post-*Everson* America.

The practice of exempting religious institutions from taxation arose in the Western world from the influence of the Bible. The Old Testament book of Ezra proclaimed, "You are also to know that you have no authority to impose taxes, tribute or duty on any of the priests, Levites, singers, gatekeepers, temple servants or other workers at this house of God."[25] European Christianity absorbed this practice, which then made its way through English law to the American colonies. At the time of the Revolutionary War, "nine of the thirteen colonies provided direct tax aid to churches."[26] Debates over the roles of church and state in the early history of the United States made little difference in a consensus that churches ought to remain tax exempt.

At the same time, few would have considered the idea of preventing churches from sounding forth on political matters. Given the comprehensive nature of colonial religion—the belief that if religion is true at all, it is true for every area of life—early generations of Americans would have found it odd indeed to restrict religion from informing politics. Throughout the American colonial experience, politics rested on a foundation of faith. An election could not be held without the clergymen of a village or township preaching Election Day sermons to assure that all citizens thought religiously about their vote. If the militia gathered, a martial sermon was preached by one or all of the ministers in a town. City councils never met, Congresses never sat, and even jails were seldom opened without sermons and prayers. The American colonists did not wish to create a government uninformed and untempered by religion. The idea of insisting that churches limit themselves to matters of faith without allowing them to speak to matters of government would have been thought foolish if not impossible.

This view prevailed both as a matter of faith and as a matter of law until well into the 1900s. Even when the counsel of the churches was divided and wrong—as in the heated disputes prior to the Civil War or when Protestants angrily opposed Roman Catholic politicians on religious grounds—the right of the churches to speak on political issues was unquestioned. Men expected, as George Santayana said, that intrusion of religion into politics "is the very work it comes into the world to do."[27]

One would expect that such an honored tradition would be altered only after a long and carefully considered process. One would expect lengthy debate, ponderous scholarship, and the most dutiful scrutiny. It was not to be. When restrictions were set upon the political speech of religious organizations, it was accomplished largely by one man and largely as a counterassault on his political enemies. This is one of the great tragedies of American political and legal history.

In 1954, Lyndon Baines Johnson was the freshman senator from Texas seeking his first reelection to office. His election to the Senate in 1948, though successful, had been so close and controversial that it had remained an embarrassment for him. He had won by a total of only eighty-seven votes—less than one hundredth of one percent of the total votes cast and this only after a mysterious "Box 13" had been produced from Duval County giving Johnson an extra two hundred votes and his opponent only one. Johnson's opponents screamed corruption and branded him with the insulting nickname "Landslide Lyndon." It was a reputation that did not die. Decades later, William Buckley Jr. would quip that his grandfather had possessed such a strong sense of "civic obligation" that though he died in 1904, he rose again to vote for Lyndon Johnson in 1948. Critics said that the elder Buckley was not the only dead man to vote for Johnson that year.

In 1954, Johnson's opponent was the largely unknown, thirty-year-old, first-term state representative from Beeville named Dudley Dougherty. Johnson did not see much of a challenge in Dougherty, whom he dubbed "the young man from Beeville." But there was another player in the game and this one Johnson feared: McCarthyism.

By 1954, the fear of communism, inspired by Senator Joseph McCarthy's hearings and speeches, had set the country on edge. As Johnson told friends in his usual earthy style, "Joe McCarthy's just a loudmouthed drunk. Hell, he's the sorriest senator up here. Can't tie his g--damn shoes. But he's riding high now, he's got people scared to death some Communist will strangle 'em in their sleep, and anybody who takes him on before the fevers cool—well, you don't get in a pissin' contest with a polecat."[28]

Johnson soon found himself walking a tightrope. He despised McCarthy but had long known that many of the big oilmen from Texas loved "Tailgunner Joe" and his stridently conservative stand. Needing the huge amounts of money these men could pour into his campaign, Johnson tempered his public opposition to McCarthy to keep their support. This seemed to work with most of the Texas oilmen—except for one.

H. L. Hunt was the brand of staunchly conservative, anticommunist that haunted Lyndon Johnson's dreams. He was more than an oilman. He was also an activist who funded a conservative, tax-exempt organization called Facts Forum. Known for producing an astonishing array of radio shows, television programs, books, and magazines, Facts Forum espoused an exceptionally hard anticommunist line. Johnson, whose approach to communism was more moderate, rightly suspected that Facts Forum was secretly supporting his opponent, Dougherty. But Facts Forum wasn't alone. Frank Gannett, owner of one of the largest newspaper chains in the country, had founded a tax-exempt organization called Committee for Constitutional Government (CCG), which was wildly successful in blanketing the country with anticommunist material. In a seven-year period, CCG had distributed more than 82 million pieces of literature, made over 100,000 radio transcripts, sent 350,000 telegrams, and issued thousands of news releases.[29] The organization was among the most powerful of its kind, and it, too, was quietly but effectively opposing the reelection of Lyndon Johnson.

Enduring political opposition from well-financed, tax-exempt organizations infuriated Johnson. He knew this growing trend was of concern to other members of Congress as well. Already there had been a House Special Committee to Investigate Tax-Exempt Foundations, but it was winding down, and Johnson wasn't satisfied with its conclusion that there was little to be done about the influence of tax-exempt organizations in politics. He decided to investigate the issue on his own. As he told a friend, "I myself am wondering whether contributions to an organization so actively engaged in politics can be classed as a legitimate corporate expense and I am having this question explored by experts."[30]

What Johnson learned was that a 1934 amendment to the statutes that governed tax-exempt organizations originally included the words "and no substantial part of the activities of which is participation in partisan politics or in carrying on propaganda, or otherwise attempting to influence legislation." When the bill was passed, though, the words "participation in partisan politics" were stricken.[31] Clearly, the earlier Congress had taken the teeth out of the law. Thus the political troubles the junior senator from Texas was having with Facts Forum and CCG.

Johnson decided to act. On July 2, 1954, the House Special Committee to Investigate Tax-Exempt Foundations ended its deliberations. That same day, Lyndon Johnson rose on the floor of the Senate and offered his amendment to the Internal Revenue Service Code pertaining to political activities by 501(c)(3) organizations. The entire affair was over in a matter of seconds. In fact, the complete transcript of what occurred is but a few paragraphs long in the *Congressional Record*:

Mr. JOHNSON of Texas: Mr. President, I have an amendment at the desk, which I should like to have stated.

The PRESIDING OFFICER: The Secretary will state the amendment.

The CHIEF CLERK: On page 117 of the House bill, in section 501(c)(3), it is proposed to strike out "individuals, and" and insert "individual," and strike out "influence legislation." And insert "influence legislation, and which does not participate in, or intervene in (including the publishing or distributing of statements), any political campaign on behalf of any candidate for public office."

Mr. JOHNSON of Texas: Mr. President, this amendment seeks to extend the provisions of section 501 of the House bill, denying tax-exempt status to not only those people who influence legislation but also to those who intervene in any political campaign on behalf of any candidate for any public office. I have discussed the matter with the chairman of the committee, the minority ranking member of the committee, and several other members of the committee, and I understand that the amendment is acceptable to them. I hope the chairman will take it to conference, and that it will be included in the final bill which Congress passes.[32]

That was it. The Republican majority accepted the amendment on unanimous consent. There were no hearings and no debate. Within moments the historic change was made. The next day, the front page of the *Washington Post* described the amendment broadly as one that "would withdraw tax-free status from any foundations or other organizations that attempt to 'influence legislation' or dabble in politics in behalf of any candidate for public office."[33]

Johnson could hardly have comprehended the long-term impact of his amendment. He had intended to restrict tax-exempt foundations from mixing in politics largely to prevent opposition to his agenda by well-funded conservatives. He does not seem to have had religion particularly in view. It doesn't matter. Johnson's amendment to the IRS code pertaining to 501(c)(3) organizations has meant that every tax-exempt church and ministry in America is kept from endorsing candidates or specific legislation if it would keep its tax-exempt status.

Those who violate the code are punished. In 1992, Pierce Creek Church in upstate New York took out an advertisement in *USA Today* and the *Washington Times* warning of Bill Clinton's support for abortion on demand, homosexual rights, and distribution of condoms in high schools. The ad asked, "How then can we vote for Bill Clinton?" For this incursion into the political arena, Pierce Creek Church lost its tax-exempt status.[34] This meant, of course, that contributions to the church were no longer tax deductible and that the church's income would decrease dramatically. It was devastating. The revoking of tax-exempt status amounts to a declaration of war on a church's future. More recently and on the other side of the political spectrum, Reverend George F. Regas of All Saints Episcopal Church in Pasadena, California, told his congregation that he could imagine Jesus Christ telling George W. Bush that his doctrine of regime change in Iraq has been a disaster. This and similar comments during a sermon have prompted the IRS to launch an aggressive investigation to determine whether the church will be allowed to retain its tax-exempt status.[35]

What makes this restriction in the tax code so insidious is that it relies for its enforcement on reporting by third parties. This means little more than religious spying. As Steve T. Miller, Director of Exempt Organizations for the Internal Revenue Service, told Congress in 2002, "In the church area we are most often left to use third party referrals of information about potential noncompliance."

Everson's army delights in filling this "third party" role. Pastors in some states, particularly those in national election swing states, are used to receiving "Dear Religious Leader" letters from Barry Lynn of Americans United for Separation of Church and State. Such letters warn against the use of voter guides, against the use of the pulpit to address political issues, and against endorsing candidates or issues lest the church lose tax-exempt status. Violators are reported to authorities in a manner reminiscent of the Nazi encouragement to "report the undesirables." Many pastors, confused by the vague restrictions, retreat further from political issues in the pulpit than even broad separationists like Barry Lynn intend. Others dare to speak the political implications of their faith, willing to risk an IRS investigation for the sake of proclaiming their version of the truth.

The greatest loss created by Johnson's amendment, though, is not to the church, as some would think, but rather to the arena of law and politics. If law is concerned with codifying a value system and politics is concerned with the just application of power, then religion is essential to both, for religion provides the ethics and guiding philosophy that both require. Without the righteous vision religion brings to the public sphere, public policy descends to mere procedure, and political leadership descends to mere engineering. Both the political process and the nation suffer in the void. This was certainly the conclusion of Martin Luther King Jr. who knew well the horrors of politics divorced from a religiously inspired vision of the righteous society:

> The church must be reminded that it is not the master or the servant of the state, but rather the conscience of the state. It must be the guide and the critic of the state, and never its tool. If the church does not recapture its prophetic zeal, it will become an irrelevant social club without moral or spiritual authority. If the church does not participate actively in the struggle for peace and for economic and racial justice, it

will forfeit the loyalty of millions and cause men everywhere to say that it has atrophied its will. But if the church will free itself from the shackles of a deadening status quo, and, recovering its great historic mission, will speak and act fearlessly and insistently in terms of justice and peace, it will enkindle the imagination of mankind and fire the souls of men, imbuing them with a glowing and ardent love for truth, justice, and peace. Men far and near will know the church as a great fellowship of love that provides light and bread for lonely travelers at midnight.[36]

5

THE RETURN

Barry Lynn, executive director of Americans United for Separation of Church and State, is concerned. He worries that if churches are allowed to speak out politically, "we're going to see politicians running around seeking support of churches and hoping that they can curry favor with those churches by promising them money and favors."[1]

Thank God, then, that Americans are protected from such misdeeds by the current laws. Or are they? Consider:

- Pastor Charles Betts Sr. at the Morningstar Missionary Baptist Church in Queens, New York, introduced First Lady Hillary Rodham Clinton, who was running for the Senate, by saying, "I would like to introduce to you the next senator." He then stated, "I speak the word and the word is truth. After she goes to the Senate, she is going to come back to our communities and say 'Thank you.'" Another pastor at a Bronx church substituted her opponent's name, Representative Rick Lazio, for Satan in a hymn sung during a visit by the First Lady.[2]

- The Reverend Jerry Falwell, preaching at the Genoa Baptist Church in Ohio, told worshipers, "You vote for the Bush of your choice." He also warned that if Al Gore was elected, "our country is going to pay a dear price." "We simply have to beat Gore," Falwell said.[3]

- In Flint, Michigan, Al Gore attended the evening service at New Jerusalem Full Baptist Church where the speaker, Kenneth

Edmonds, urged congregants to kneel at bedtime and pray: "The Lord is my shepherd, I shall not vote for George Bush."[4]

- In Milwaukee, Wisconsin, the Reverend Joseph Noonan of Our Lady of the Rosary Roman Catholic Church urged against candidates who were not pro-life and instructed, "I'm not telling you who to vote for. I'm telling you who you may not vote for."[5]

- During Sabbath services at University Synagogue in West Los Angeles, Rabbi Allen Freehling spoke of Noah's drunkenness and remarked that the same "obscene behavior can be said of a certain Republican presidential candidate," a reference to George Bush.[6]

- President Bill Clinton spoke from the pulpit of a Harlem church to a group of African-American religious leaders and urged them that if they want to "keep the economy going" then "you have to vote for Hillary and Al Gore and Joe Lieberman."[7]

- In Miami, twenty-three ministers met in the Jordan Grove Baptist Church to coordinate efforts to get out the vote for Al Gore. They agreed to do radio ads, to coordinate vans to get people to the polls, and pledged to preach from the pulpit about voting. John Sales of First Baptist of Brownsville explained: "You don't have to need someone to tell you to vote. We've got to watch out for what's in the Bushes."[8]

- In Chicago, about twenty ministers boycotted the *Chicago Sun-Times* for its endorsement of George Bush for president. The ministers said they will now rely on their pulpits and other newspapers to keep their communities informed about the elections.[9]

- In Detroit, Al Gore told a Sunday congregation, "I need you to lift me up so I can fight for you." He was introduced by the church's pastor, Bishop Charles H. Ellis III, who offered a prayer for Mr. Gore's success and told his congregation that the choice "seems to be a no-brainer to me—if it ain't broke, don't fix it."[10]

- In Arkansas, Kathy Robinson, a Democratic activist, complained about a county clerk refusing to open the clerk's office for early voting on Sunday, explaining, "I had seventeen Afro-American churches lined up to be bused to the courthouse to vote on Sunday." She then added, "Now I am going to have to retract that. We are trying to get Gore elected."[11]

In each of these episodes, a violation of the Internal Revenue Service Code for 501(c)(3) organizations occurred. In each, a church endorsed a political candidate. In each, religion stepped into the arena of politics.

And the Republic still stands.

WE LIVE IN AN AGE OF FAITH AND YET AN AGE WHEN FAITH IS feared. We live at a time when men yearn to believe and yet doubt those who do. We live in a day when religion lifts men to greatness but also makes them vicious and hard, when a vision of God makes nations noble but also leads to unspeakable horror.

It is, as Dickens said, "the best of times and the worst of times," and for very much the same reason that this was true in his day: crises of faith lead to crises of culture, and so it is in America.

What distinguishes the crises of faith in our day, though, is that they are often rooted more in fear of faith than in lack of faith. Earlier generations who moved away from traditional faith simply chose not to believe. They did not fear religion; they quietly concluded that religion wasn't true. We dare to believe religion might be true but fear the consequences.

Yet our generation has been given good reason to suspect faith. After all, Feuerbach told us that man created God and not the other way around, Freud told us that God is a projection of man's own psychology, Marx told us that religion is like opium, and Nietzsche told us there is no God but that in His absence the State will do just fine. This was all before various New Age religions told us that we are God.

What we see in the world around us doesn't help. A Pennsylvania milkman shoots ten Amish schoolchildren because he is angry with God for the death of his child. While he is murdering six-year-old farm girls, his wife is attending a Presbyterian prayer meeting to ask God's protection for the children of their town. Held up against the daily slaughter of dozens worldwide in the name of Allah, the confessions of murderers who claim God told them to kill, and the passing parade of bizarre behavior in the name of religion, it is all enough to induce madness. Or anger, and this seems to be where many in our culture have settled: anger at any public manifestation of religion.

Consider a response to what happened on the floor of Congress in September of 2006. The task at hand was passing the National Defense Authorization Act of 2007, a measure that determined fiscal appropriations for the nation's defense. The business of the House stalled, though, when debate turned to the question of whether military chaplains should be permitted to pray in the name of Jesus Christ, or, as press reports phrased it, pray "sectarian prayers." Representatives Todd Akin of Missouri, Randy Forbes of Virginia, and Walter Jones of North Carolina had been contending for some time that unwarranted restrictions prevented chaplains from praying as their faiths dictated in military assemblies. These restrictions had been tightened in 2004 after allegations of proselytizing and religious coercion arose at the United States Air Force Academy. Conservatives in the House held up passage of the appropriations act in hopes of modifying what they deemed excessive restrictions on the freedom of chaplains to express their faith.

Debate in the House grew heated on the subject, the deadline for recess neared, and a compromise was struck. The tightened restrictions spawned by the Air Force Academy affair were lifted, but no new freedoms regarding prayer were granted.

What astounds is the anger the proposed measures incited. Lieutenant Colonel Robert Bateman, a serving infantry officer, strategist, and military historian who spent a year in Iraq, declared himself on the matter even before Congress acted:

> As a professional officer, should such a law be passed, my solution is simple in the extreme. I will stop allowing chaplains to give prayers in public military ceremonies or events in which I am involved.
>
> There are, after all, no regulations that require the military to allow the chaplains to give a moment of prayer at the opening of one of these events . . . So, if I am a commander, I just dump the chaplain. He can still have his office, his position, his weekly prayer service in any spot he can find, and access to the troops if they choose to come to him. But he won't be giving public prayers at any military functions for me anymore, regardless of his denomination, because I cannot afford the possibility that he might accuse me of religious bias in favor of one sect or another. Because there are now more evangelical Christian ministers, this will naturally damage their efforts more than any other sect, but such is the law of unintended consequences.[12]

Clearly, Lt. Col. Bateman would rather "dump the chaplain" and the good done for the troops than allow servicemen to hear prayers based on faiths different from their own. Yet this is in the grand military tradition. Chaplains have long ministered to servicemen who were not of the same faith, and tales of such deference to the religions of others forms part of the noble heritage of the chaplains' corps.

One brief story suffices to prove the point. During World War II, the American transport ship *Dorchester* was steaming through the icy North Atlantic in waters dubbed "Torpedo Junction" because of the hundreds of ships sunk there each month. Aboard were four chaplains—two Protestant, one Catholic, and one Jewish—who had become close friends at chaplains' school. This bonding led them to pray together often and gave them a familiarity with each other's faiths that served their men well. It was not uncommon for a Catholic soldier to call for a chaplain and find the Rabbi at his side reciting the Hail Mary or the Our Father.

On the night of February 3, 1943, a German submarine scored a direct hit on the *Dorchester* just below the waterline. She was certain to sink and the order to abandon ship was given. When all lifeboats were launched, the men realized that the four chaplains had decided to go down with the ship. Linking arms and grasping the railing, the four chaplains began shouting to the men in the sea. But it was what the chaplains yelled that bears remembering.

Above the moans and cries of grief, soldiers in the lifeboats or floating in the water could hear their four chaplains singing and shouting encouragement together. First they heard the Lord's Prayer in English. Then they heard all four men—the Protestants, the Catholic, and the Jew—calling out the *Shema* in Hebrew: "*Shema Yisrael, Adonai eloheinu, Adonai echad*"—"Hear, O Israel, the Lord thy God, the Lord thy God is one." Latin was next, with the priest leading the way in portions of the Catholic Mass. When all this was done, the chaplains would preach faith in God to their perishing men and then return to the ancient words of comfort from all their faiths. Private First Class William Bednar, floating among his dead comrades, later said, "Their voices were the only thing that kept me going." Finally, twenty-seven minutes after the torpedo hit, the *Dorchester* slipped beneath the waves, taking the four chaplains to their deaths in the deep.

This episode is not an isolated and now forgotten event. There is a chapel window commemorating the *Dorchester* chaplains at the United States Military Academy at West Point and one equally stunning at the Pentagon. Ministering across lines of faith is an honored and revered tradition in the American military chaplains' corps, but Lt. Col. Bateman would "dump the chaplain" in fear that a soldier might hear a prayer from a faith other than his own. Both the military and the nation would be poorer for the choice.

Equally astonishing is the anger of Christopher Hitchens, esteemed columnist for *Vanity Fair*. Because he is an articulate journalist, a gifted scholar, and a recent convert to political conservativism, his response to the debate over chaplains' prayers is particularly revealing. Writing for Slate.com, Hitchens charged that the actions of the three representatives—Akin, Forbes, and Jones—hindered passage of the military appropriations measure and amounted to a "clear and present danger to the national defense and ought to be regarded and treated as such."[13]

These are harsh words and they border on charging the congressmen with treason, but the more critical case is the one Hitchens makes from history. "Why are there official chaplains in the armed forces at all?" he demands. "Is not their very presence, paid for out of the public treasury, an affront to the establishment clause of the all-important First Amendment? The author of that amendment, James Madison, certainly thought so. His 'Detached Memorandum,' which also opposed the use of chaplains to open the proceedings of the Congress, were very clear about clerics in the armed forces."[14]

Hitchens gives voice to just the tone of historical distortion merged with anger at religion that typifies many in our present culture. He is opposed to religion and wishes the founding fathers were, as well. They weren't. Even Madison, who did indeed oppose both military and congressional chaplains in the "Detached Memorandum" of his latter years, understood the value of religion to the new Republic. "Religion is the basis and foundation of government," he once proclaimed, and thus he not only served on the committee that appointed chaplains when he was in Congress but also voted to set chaplains' salaries within days of helping to ratify the First Amendment.[15] This ought to forever solve the question of whether chaplains are inconsistent with the Establishment Clause, as Hitchens asserts. They aren't. Moreover, Hitchens makes his case, as secularists often do, from the words of Madison alone. But what of the other 125 founding fathers? Why are their views ignored in deference to Madison? He no more embodied the thinking of his generation than did any other single founding father. Indeed, perhaps less so. Clearly, Hitchens's historical case is found wanting, but perhaps the more central matter is his offense that religion has presumed to influence public policy at all.

This popular—and often understandable—animosity toward religion, fueled as it usually is by just enough historical misrepresentation, is certainly one of the cultural legacies of the *Everson* ruling. If, as Justice Black argued, the founding fathers intended no public role for religion—no support for faith of any kind by government at any level—then religion in the public square is an interloper, an intruder illegally attempting a coup. It should be resented, hated, and opposed. It is, according to this view, out of line with the vision of the founding fathers, inconsistent with the American way, and sure to destroy democracy. No wonder, then, the animosity of Bateman and Hitchens. No wonder, then, the suspicion of the religious.

This perspective—that the founders intended a secular State that religion now invades—explains much of the pettiness that attends the opposition to religion in American public life. We must take a moment to realize that we are not dealing today with the grand issues of religious tyranny that the founders faced. They labored to prevent the continuance of an Anglican-style State church in America. No one of serious mind today is advocating such a thing. There is no movement for an American State church. Indeed, no one is calling for the

Baptist State of Georgia or the Muslim Republic of Michigan, either. The truth is that nothing of the type of religious establishment the founders sought to prevent is even a remote threat now.

Instead, what passes for a victory against religious establishments today is the removing of a tiny cross from a county seal. Great blows for liberty are thought to be struck when schoolchildren are kept from asking whose birthday is celebrated on Christmas or when military chaplains are told how to pray. Indeed, the miniscule nature of the typical Establishment Clause complaint is an embarrassment: a cross in a cemetery, two words in a pledge, a book on a teacher's desk, the mentioning of a Creator for a few minutes after weeks of public classroom instruction in evolution, the singing of Christmas carols, a locker room moment of silence before a high school football game. If these define the battle against religious establishment in our time, then we have no battle of consequence to fight.

What we do have is a culture of religious mean-spiritedness. A Christian man drives down a road and notices the crescent, a symbol of Islam, adorning the entrance to a state cemetery. It is a monument in honor of Muslim-American soldiers who fought and died in the Iraq war. Does the man pause to consider what these soldiers endured, how they may have wrestled with fighting against people of their own faith, and how they gave all for a nation that did not always welcome them? No. He considers only that the symbol of a faith he does not approve of is standing on public land. On the basis of a First Amendment that says nothing about the matter, he files a complaint asserting that government can't fund religion. The symbol is removed, and Muslim-American soldiers are dishonored.

Why? Was this crescent a serious attempt to establish the Muslim faith as the official religion of a state or federal government? Was the Christian man harmed in any way? Was he kept from worshipping as he wished, forced to believe something at odds with his chosen faith, or made to honor a God not his own? No. He just didn't like the crescent, and the culture of *Everson* allows him, on that basis alone, to dishonor American servicemen in the name of religious liberty.

What is tragically forgotten is that the most promising path for true religious liberty, particularly the version embraced by those concerned about religious establishments, is the one that leads to a religious free market. This has provided the most religious freedom for the most Americans in the past and may again if the tyrannies of misguided laws are lifted.

Let us recall that when the *Everson* case was decided in 1947, there were no established state churches to overturn. Not one state still mandated an official religion. Where were the established churches of earlier American history, then? The answer is that the states had decided on their own to dismantle them.

Consider that at the outbreak of the American Revolution in 1775, nine of the thirteen colonies had established churches.[16] At that time, the Anglican Church had been established "in Virginia in 1609, in New York's lower counties in 1693, in Maryland in 1702, in South Carolina in 1706, in North Carolina nominally in 1711, and in Georgia in 1758. The Congregational Church was established in Massachusetts, Connecticut, and New Hampshire."[17] By the time that the Constitutional Convention assembled in Philadelphia in 1787, only five of these nine establishments remained: Georgia, South Carolina, Connecticut, Massachusetts, and New Hampshire. The other four states had voluntarily disestablished religion, as would Connecticut in 1818, New Hampshire in 1819, and Massachusetts in 1833.[18] No action by the federal government or courts was required. States disestablished official religions because that is what the people wished.

It is here that we see the best guarantee of religious liberty. The truth is that a Republic achieves the greatest freedom when the will of the people is expressed through their elected leaders and through unfettered choices in a free market. This is as true of religion as it is of any matter of politics or economics. It may well be that the best hedge against an unconstitutional establishment of religion is the will of the people expressing itself in a religious free market. Clearly, the people did not wish religious establishment to remain in the nine states that had them at the time of the Revolution. In addition, none of the states that came into the Union thereafter chose official religions. The people preferred that no one religion be set above another but that religion in general should be encouraged by government. This was, not surprisingly, precisely what the founding fathers had envisioned from the beginning.

Indeed, many of the concerns expressed today about religion in politics might well be addressed by the public being left to vote with their feet. Barry Lynn is concerned that churches allowed to endorse candidates and specific legislation will become targets of corruption and may become centers of political activism under the guise of religion. Yet, while trends indicate that most people want their churches to speak meaningfully to matters of politics, parishioners would likely leave a church that focused on politics alone. Any pastor who rammed his political opinions down the throats of his congregation as though these opinions came from God would surely lose support. Here again, the natural corrections of a market work in religion as they do in other spheres.

The same is true not only of an emphasis on politics in general in a church but also of a particular political leaning, as well. The wise pastor knows that he may teach the implications of his faith for the political arena but that unreserved endorsement of either political party will frustrate most congregants. The people want to be taught the truth and then left to decide. Churches that mandate political views on the same level as religious doctrine would likely face serious crisis. Over time, with this lesson learned, churches would avoid by choice the pitfalls Barry Lynn fears. In the meantime, churches speaking broadly to questions of politics and public policy would bring fresh sea winds of wisdom to government and political leadership.

It is precisely to assure such a free market of religion that a number of historic measures are presently working their way through Congress. An example is HR 235, the Houses of Worship Free Speech Restoration Act.

The act's sponsor is Congressman Walter Jones of North Carolina's third district. Far from the fire-breathing stalwart of the Religious Right one might expect, Jones speaks with a gentle Carolina accent reminiscent of Old South gentility. He is a convert to Catholicism, an unswerving political conservative, and an independent thinker seemingly immune to the "group think" on Capitol Hill. Though he once backed George W. Bush's entrance into the war in Iraq, Jones has broken from the pro-war pack and joined Congressmen Neil Abercrombie, Dennis Kucinich, and Ron Paul in calling for the withdrawal of US forces.

What launched Jones into the politics of religion was a letter written in October 2000 by Barry Lynn of Americans United for Separation of Church and State. It was a typical "Dear Religious Leader" letter of the kind Lynn is known for sending. Still, it incensed Jones. The letter asserted that "houses of worship, as non-profit entities under Section 501(c)(3) of the Internal Revenue Service Tax Code, are barred from endorsing or opposing candidates for any public office and may not intervene directly or indirectly in partisan campaigns." It went on to question the ethics of Pat Robertson's Christian Coalition and to threaten the loss of tax-exempt status for churches that distributed the Coalition's voter guides.[19]

Jones soon learned that Americans United intended to mail the letter to more than 285,000 houses of worship, which, according to Lynn, would reach "nearly 90% of the nation's total. I'm confident that every church targeted by the Coalition will receive this letter." The partisan intent of the mailing was obvious to Jones from an Americans United press release of September 28, 2000.

> These documents [the Coalition's voter guides] are not voter guides at all. Instead, they are partisan campaign fliers that advocate the election of certain candidates and the defeat of others . . . The Coalition's 75 million voter guides don't belong in church bulletins or in the lobbies of our houses of worship. They belong at the local recycling center or landfill. Our new Project is designed to ensure that they end up there . . . We believe our Letter to churches will bring their [the Christian Coalition's] misguided voter guide project to a screeching halt. We're throwing a monkey wrench into Pat Robertson's political machine.[20]

Reading the press release led to a defining moment for the North Carolina congressman. He already knew how Lyndon Johnson had engineered a change in the IRS code to keep tax-exempt organizations from political speech. He knew that even though Johnson had not intended to target religion, his amendment now restricted every 501(c)(3) religious organization in the country. And here, in Barry Lynn's letter, he saw how the game is played, how a group like Americans United could threaten thousands of churches along partisan lines. That was when Walter Jones determined that something had to change.

He decided to partner with House and Senate colleagues to sponsor a bill that would remove the political restrictions on houses of worship from the IRS tax code. Known now as the Houses of Worship Free Speech Restoration Act, it would allow religious leaders around the country to speak freely to all matters of government and politics without fear of losing their tax-exempt status. As Congressman Jones has said from the floor of the House:

From the beginning of America until 1954, there was never any restriction of speech on our churches, synagogues and mosques in this country, never until the Johnson amendment that went through the Senate on a revenue bill, never debated. Now ministers, priests and rabbis have the Federal Government through the Internal Revenue Service looking in on what they have to say when they are before their congregation.

Madam Speaker, I think that is a sad commentary on America. I think it is a sad commentary on those who have worn the uniform for this Nation and fought for freedom for the American people.

If this was 1953, I would not be before this House because there would be no problem, there would be no restriction of speech. The first amendment right would be protected for those who speak on behalf of their Lord. Madam Speaker, I close by saying that I hope that those of us in Congress on both sides of the aisle will do our part to make sure that the first amendment right applies to those who are spiritual leaders of America and protect their rights for which men and women have worn the uniform or are wearing the uniform.[21]

Walter Jones first proposed his bill in 2001 and has fought hard to bring it to a vote. He finds that even the leadership of his own party is slow to embrace the bill, largely because of the political price. But Jones is undaunted. "This is now my central mission," he contends. "In fact, this may be the main reason I've been placed in Congress. If I can help free the houses of worship in this country so that they can again be the conscience of the state, I will consider it a huge victory for the nation."

A second bill, the Public Expression of Religion Act (HR 2769), is often deemed a holy cause by its supporters as well. Intended to ban fee shifting in Establishment Clause cases, the bill began making its way through Congress in May of 2005 and by September of 2006 had already passed the House of Representatives. This was a victory due in large part to aggressive lobbying by Rees Lloyd and the American Legion, who placed passage of the bill at the top of its agenda as a defense of fundamental American liberties.

The bill's sponsor was Representative John Hostetler of Indiana's eighth district. Tall and commanding with a gentle but business-like manner, Hostetler first gained a vision for what America had been and could be again from listening to Dr. D. James Kennedy's radio broadcast, *Truths That Transform*. When Bill Clinton took office in 1992, the Indiana engineer saw the country beginning to move in a very different direction from the founding dream Kennedy so often described. Hostetler ran for office, won, and then began to realize anew the damage that Establishment Clause lawsuits coupled with fee shifting was visiting on the nation.[22]

He launched a vigorous campaign to educate his fellow congressmen on the issue. His success is evident in a Judiciary Committee press release distributed prior to hearings on the new bill in June of 2005:

The Supreme Court has stated "the State may not establish a religion of secularism in the sense of affirmatively opposing or showing hostility to religion, thus preferring those who believe in no religion over those who do believe." However, contrary to that principle, current litigation rules are stacked against religious expression because those rules allow some groups to coerce States and localities into removing any reference to religion in public places.

CURRENTLY . . .
- Federal law allows people to sue the state or local governments for alleged constitutional violations of their individual rights. Consequently, any individual or group could sue a state or local government claiming their individual rights were violated and

demand attorneys' fees in the case if they prevail at any stage of judicial review.

- Fearing the high cost of paying not only their own legal fees to fight the case but also the attorneys' fees of the plaintiffs, many localities without deep pockets are coerced to simply cave to demands to remove religious expression from the public square.

- Los Angeles County is spending around $1 million to remove a tiny cross from the official county seal (symbolizing the founding of the County by missionaries), fearing the cost of litigation to defend the tiny seal. Thus, the seal now must be changed on approximately 90,000 uniforms, 6,000 buildings, and 12,000 county vehicles.

HR 2679 WILL . . .

Amend current law to prohibit the awarding of monetary damages and/or attorneys' fees to prevailing parties in cases involving the Constitution's Establishment Clause. This will prevent the use of the legal system in a manner that coerces money from State and local governments and inhibits their constitutional actions, including religious expression.

Part of what made Hostetler so convincing was his fair-mindedness. He did not defend his bill in a "protect-religious-expression-at-all-costs" spirit of the kind that so often attends such efforts. Instead, he explained that fee shifting routinely prevented many Establishment Clause cases from ever being tried. The threat of paying the legal bills for both sides of a suit usually persuaded defendants to surrender principle and settle out of court, which meant that religious speech was routinely silenced without challenge. Hostetler believed this was contrary to the American way and told his fellow congressmen that he merely wanted justice not preference, that Establishment Clause cases ought to be tried openly and fairly in court. This was all his bill would accomplish, he explained. His reasoning prevailed, convincing enough House members to pass the measure by a vote of 244–173. The companion bill in the Senate (S 3696), if passed, will finally remove the advantage that ACLU-type organizations have enjoyed in Establishment Clause litigation since 1976.

A third strategy for assuring religious liberty in recent years is one that seeks to prevent courts from ruling on certain types of religion cases altogether. Represented by bills like the We the People Act (HR 5739), sponsored by Representative Ron Paul of Texas, and the Constitution Restoration Act (S 520, HR 1070), sponsored by Senator Shelby and Representative Aderholt, both of Alabama, these bills call for the exercise of a congressional prerogative that few Americans are even aware exists.

Article III, Section 2, of the US Constitution gives authority to Congress to determine what kind of cases may be heard before the federal courts. In this Exceptions Clause, Congress is allowed to make exceptions to the range of cases the courts would normally hear. It does not happen often, but in issues ranging from slavery just prior to the Civil War to more recent matters of environmental protections, Congress has from time to time restricted the courts from hearing cases in a specific category of law.

This is what these more recent bills seek to do in certain matters of religion. The We the People Act, for example, would require that "the Supreme Court of the United States and each Federal court shall not adjudicate any claim involving the laws, regulations, or policies of any State or unit of local government relating to the free exercise or establishment of religion," among other provisions. The Constitution Restoration Act would insist that "the Supreme Court shall not have jurisdiction to review, by appeal, writ of certiorari, or otherwise, any matter to the extent that relief is sought against an entity of Federal, State, or local government, concerning that entity's, officer's, or agent's acknowledgement of God as the sovereign source of law, liberty, or government."

These efforts are not the first time that the Exceptions Clause has been employed in an attempt to protect religious rights. In 1979 and again in 1981, Senator Jesse Helms attempted to activate the Exceptions Clause to prevent federal courts from ruling on matters of school prayer. His bill would have blocked "any case arising out of any State statute, ordinance, rule, regulation, practice, or any part thereof, or arising out of any Act interpreting, applying, enforcing, or effecting any State statute, ordinance, rule, regulation or practice, which relates to voluntary prayer, Bible reading, or religious meetings in public schools or public buildings."[23] This and similar measures that Helms proposed in the ensuing years failed to gain momentum, but the hope of using the Exceptions Clause to restrict courts from certain types of Establishment Clause cases never died. Even if the We the People Act and the Constitution Restoration Act should fail to garner support, it is likely new measures of this kind will continue to appear.

The appeal of restricting courts from certain categories of law pertaining to religion is that it leaves decisions regarding the role of religion in American public life with elected legislatures. Rather than the Supreme Court deciding matters of school prayer or religious symbols on public property, for example, these decisions would be made by the US Congress and the state legislatures. Critics charge that this would likely leave a religious patchwork throughout the nation, with one state allowing prayer before its legislative sessions and another forbidding it, one state permitting religious symbols on public property and the very next state banning them. Yet those who support an

Exceptions Clause approach to these issues contend that not only would these critical decisions be made by elected officials accountable to the people but also that such a religious patchwork is exactly what the founding fathers intended when they prohibited the federal government from establishing religion but kept the states religiously free to fulfill the will of the people.

Each of these efforts—to allow political speech to tax-exempt organizations, to ban fee shifting in Establishment Clause cases, and to restrict courts from certain cases involving religion—are recent attempts to restore what has been lost to the nation through the misreading of the founders' purpose in the Establishment Clause. Should all of them fail to become law, others like them will surely arise. The sense in the nation that something has gone horribly wrong in matters of religion and government is too pronounced for the current status quo to remain much longer.

Indeed, pressure for change in these areas may come from a surprising source in the near future. For the last three to four decades, opposition to the legacy of *Everson* has come largely from the conservative side of the political spectrum, the Religious Right in particular. It is this political segment that has held forth for State-supported, faith-based social action, for greater religious expression in schools, for wider latitude for state and federal governments to honor religion, and for the voice of faith to be heard in the political process.

Surprisingly, this pressure may soon come from the political left, or from what some are calling the "Religious Left." The fact is that the religious heritage of liberalism is being rediscovered today, and this may dramatically transform the traditional battle lines that have long pitted the Religious Right against the Secular Left. Liberals like Jimmy Carter, Tony Campolo, and Jim Wallis are calling for a faith-based politic of the left and are receiving a widespread hearing. The heritage of faith-based liberalism—of Martin Luther King Jr.'s social activism of Dorothy Day and the Catholic Worker Movement, of William Sloane Coffin's Peace Action—is being reclaimed. And the lessons of recent elections speed this process: American voters look for leaders comfortable with faith and clear on values. Already the nation is hearing Hillary Clinton defend her immigration policy from the words of Jesus and liberal congressmen oppose the war in Iraq with quotes from the Old Testament prophets. The next presidential election promises to be a contest of religious worldviews as much as, if not more than, any other in American history.

Strengthening this trend are the political leanings of a rising new generation. The Millennials, those who came of age around the dawn of the new millennium and are now in their early to middle twenties, delight in blurring traditional lines. Just as in religion they eschew church but pursue God, love religious community but despise religious formality, the Millennials are also defying definitions in politics. They clearly yearn for a politic shaped by religious values, yet they are broad about what those values should be. Many wonder why the politics of Teddy Kennedy should be regarded as any less religiously based than that of George W. Bush. Why should Kennedy's Catholic liberalism not be viewed as "faith-based" when Bush's evangelical conservatism wears that label gladly? The Millennials, ever the innovators, will almost certainly call for a new blend of politics and religion and yet of a kind that is destined to frustrate both sides of the current political spectrum. The nation will likely be richer for it.

What is certain is that with 82 percent of Americans affirming faith in God, with voters displaying a clear preference for a religion-inspired political vision, and with global events pressing matters of faith to the fore, the secularizing trend of recent decades is likely to dwindle if not die.[24] Then, perhaps, the wisdom of the American founding fathers will be consulted anew. If so, the ten words of the

Establishment Clause will cease being tortured into a challenge to religion and become instead the well-defined boundary for government that allows religion to ennoble the life of the nation, just as the American founders dared to hope.

EPILOGUE

The year was 1945 and the Western Allies had just defeated the forces of the Third Reich. Germany lay devastated. To help her rebuild as a free society and to assure there would be no Nazi uprising, the Allies partitioned Germany into zones of responsibility. The Americans took a portion of the south, the French a swath along the western border, the British a northwest section that jutted into the sea, and the Russians an eastern quarter surrounding Berlin.

Berlin. She had been the prize, the capital of the Nazi empire. The Allies divided her too. Since the Russians led the assault on the Nazi capital and had suffered staggering losses during the war, they were given nearly the entire eastern half of the city. The French, the British, and the Americans each shared a third of the western half. There were tensions, of course. In 1948, the Russians hoped to starve the Allies out of the city, and so they cut off supply routes. Since Berlin lay deep in the heart of the Russian zone of Germany, this was easy for the Soviets to do. The genius of the Berlin Airlift, led largely by the Americans, broke the Soviet stranglehold, though. Planes landed at a rate of one every two minutes and supplied the needs of the city for eleven months. Finally, in May of 1949, the Soviets saw the futility of their plan and lifted the blockade.

Though tensions between Eastern and Western blocs would continue over the next decade, the borders between the two halves of the city would remain open. This was the problem. The Socialist world wasn't working economically, and East Germany—that section ruled by the Soviets—was losing more than a hundred thousand people a year, three-quarters of them through Berlin. These refugees wanted the promise of the West, but the drain on the East was something its leaders could not allow. More doctors were leaving the East than could be trained to replace them. More technicians too. The situation could not continue.

The Soviet solution descended on August 13, 1961. Under cover of darkness, at midnight on a Sunday, Russian and East German soldiers began nailing barbed wire to posts strewn along a 5.6 mile section of the border between East and West Berlin. The city awoke to the confusing news. No one seemed to understand what it meant at first. As the soldiers worked with lightning speed over the following weeks, the confusion cleared and the horrifying realization dawned: the West was being cut off.

Before long, a twenty-six-mile-long barrier lay between the Russian and Allied sectors of the city. There was more, though. The Soviets had also erected a sixty-nine-mile barrier around the borders of the Allied sectors. This barrier, like the one that zigzagged through the middle of the city, was more than a wall. It was a hundred-meter-wide "Death Strip" of barbed wire, tank traps, dogs, and guard towers with machine guns jutting in every direction. In a matter of weeks, West Berlin had become an angrily guarded island in a Soviet sea.

It would remain so for the next twenty-eight years. Though the vicious scar of a wall would be improved from time to time—with lasers replacing barbed wire in some sections or mines replacing tank traps—the message was always the same. Freedom had borders—deadly borders at which human life and dignity had no meaning.

There were escape attempts, of course. Some men tried to tunnel underneath the ninety-five-mile insult to liberty, and some tried to bash their way through it. There was a famous attempt to float over it in a balloon. One man planned to catapult himself to freedom until friends talked him out of it. And many were killed. Berliners near the wall often awoke to the sound of machine-gun fire in the night, and they learned to search the papers during the following days to see if someone they knew had been killed in pursuit of freedom.

It might have lasted forever. When Soviet and East German officials celebrated the two-and-a-half decades of their "Anti-Fascist Protection Barrier" in 1986, a twenty-five-year-old Berliner—who had never known the city without the wall—could be forgiven for assuming it would all never end. The next year, Ronald Reagan issued an historic challenge in Berlin, calling upon the Soviet Premier to "tear down this wall." Crowds cheered but had good reason for thinking it might never happen.

Then it did. On November 9, 1989, officials in the East announced the end of "travel restrictions" between the two Berlins. Immediately, throngs from the East poured through the three checkpoints that led to the West. Guards were overwhelmed. That evening, crowds in the West began chipping away at the hated barrier. There were tears of joy and anger. While some West Berliners danced on top of the wall, others hacked away at the concrete with hammers and pickaxes. Before long, the guards in the East joined them, first unofficially and then under orders.

And the wall came down.

Already, the memory of it is receding into history. Today, where the Death Strip once taunted, Daimler-Benz and Sony boast soaring office buildings. People walk with ease through the Brandenburg Gate where once such a stroll meant certain death. The wall itself is nearly gone too, though some large sections made their way to the West—to the headquarters of the CIA, to the Reagan Library, and even to a urinal in a Las Vegas casino. Most of it, though, was ground into gravel and used to pave the sidewalks and roads of Berlin. Fittingly, future generations will grind this bulwark of oppression underfoot.

It will not be long before those who had known nothing but the wall in 1989 will take their grandchildren to museums to show them that it was all true. There really was a ninety-five-mile barrier between freedom and tyranny, and it really did last for nearly thirty years. And, yes, men and women gave their lives to defy it. This is what freedom means.

Today, there is another wall whose time has come to an end. It is an American wall, the one men built to guard their dreams of a secular State.

We must be clear, though. This is not the wall that stands between the institutions of religion and State. This wall we wish to keep. Few Americans hope for a government run by clergy or institutions of faith run from the corridors of political power. We leave such skewed dreams to the Taliban, to the minions of Osama bin Laden.

No, this other wall is the one that is assumed to stand between all government and all religion in this land. It is a wall built on an irrational fear of faith, one designed to keep the wells of religion from refreshing the often arid realms of government.

This wall would keep a people from honoring the faiths that built their nation as well as the faiths that join them anew. This wall would keep schools from teaching what is possibly the most important motive to human behavior—what a people believe about God and the meaning of life. This wall prevents the wisdom of the ages from being distilled into principles for governing with nobility and skill.

But this wall is only sixty years old. Like the Berlin Wall, it seems as though it will last forever. Like the Berlin Wall, it, too, is all a generation has known.

And like the Berlin Wall, it, too, may fall, leaving its rubble to pave the way for the vision of the founders: a nation that separates the institutions of religion and government but welcomes the riches of faith into the public square. This is the dream of a new generation and not because they wish to religiously oppress their neighbors. Instead, they know that the secular State has been tried and found wanting in their time, and they wish for an age in which, as Dr. King dared to hope, religion once again becomes the conscience of the State.

APPENDIX 1

THE FATHERS ON FAITH AND GOVERNMENT: TWENTY ESSENTIAL QUOTES

The debate over the religious vision of the American founders often descends into a battle of quotes. Alone, of course, quotes prove little. Men change throughout their lives, having opinions in youth they abandon with age. Men also say one thing in private correspondence and do quite another while in public office. It is dangerous to assume that one quote captures the entire thinking of a man or a generation.

That said, it has become a common assumption in our time that the founding fathers were personally religious but wished their government to be secular. Nothing could be further from the truth. The quotes below, held up against the broader material in this book, provide compelling evidence that the founding generation understood—as they wrote in the Northwest Ordinance of 1787—that "religion" is "necessary to good government."

1. *Statesmen, my dear Sir, may plan and speculate for liberty, but it is Religion and Morality alone, which can establish the Principles upon which Freedom can securely stand.* —JOHN ADAMS

   [Charles Francis Adams, ed., *The Works of John Adams—Second President of the United States*, Vol. IX, (Boston: Little, Brown, & Co., 1854), p. 401.]

2. *Religion and Virtue are the only Foundations, not only of Republicanism and of all free Government, but of social felicity under all Governments and in all Combinations of human Society.* —JOHN ADAMS

   [To Benjamin Rush, August 28, 1811. Old Family Letters, p. 354.]

3. *Our constitution was made only for a moral and religious people. It is wholly inadequate to the government of any other.* —JOHN ADAMS

[To the Officers of the First brigade of the 3rd Division of the Massachusetts Militia, October 11, 1789. *Adams Papers*, Microfilm, reel 119 Library of Congress.]

4. *From the day of the Declaration . . . they [the American people] were bound by the laws of God, which they all, and by the laws of the Gospel, which they nearly all, acknowledged as the rules of their conduct.* —JOHN QUINCY ADAMS

[John Wingate Thornton, *The Pulpit of the American Revolution 1860* (New York: Burt Franklin, 1860, 1970), p. xxix.]

5. *Our country should be preserved from the dreadful evil of becoming enemies to the religion of the Gospel, which I have no doubt, but would be the introduction of the dissolution of government and the bonds of civil society.* —ELIAS BOUDINOT

[Elias Boudinot, *The Age of Revelation* (Philadelphia: Asbury Dickins, 1801), p. xxii.]

6. *Without morals a republic cannot subsist any length of time; they therefore, who are decrying the Christian religion, whose morality is so sublime and pure, which denounces against the wicked, the eternal misery, and insures to the good eternal happiness, are undermining the solid foundations of morals, the best security for the duration of free governments.* —CHARLES CARROLL

[Alf J. Mapp Jr., *The Faiths of Our Fathers* (Lanham, MD: Rowman & Littlefield, 2003), pp. 140–41.]

7. *Religion is of general and public concern, and on its support depend, in great measure, the peace and good order of government, the safety and happiness of the people. By our form of government, the Christian religion is the established religion; and all sects and denominations of Christians are placed upon the same equal footing, and are equally entitled to protection in their religious liberty.* —SAMUEL CHASE

[*Runkel v. Winemill*, 4 Harris & McHenry 276, 288 (Sup. Ct. Md. 1799).]

8. *History will also afford frequent opportunities of showing the necessity of a public religion, from its usefulness to the public.* —BENJAMIN FRANKLIN

[Benjamin Franklin, "Proposals Relating to the Education of Youth in Pennsylvania," *Papers of Benjamin Franklin* 3 (1749): p. 413.]

9. *Whoever shall introduce into public affairs the principles of primitive Christianity will change the face of the world.* —BENJAMIN FRANKLIN

[Burton Stevenson, *The Home Book of Quotations—Classical & Modern* (New York: Dodd, Mead and Company, 1967), p. 265.]

10. *No human society has ever been able to maintain both order and freedom, both cohesiveness and liberty apart from the moral precepts of the Christian Religion applied and accepted by all the*

classes. Should our Republic ever forget this fundamental precept of governance, men are certain to shed their responsibilities for licentiousness and this great experiment will then surely be doomed.
—JOHN JAY

[Address to the American Bible Society, May 9, 1822, in *The Correspondence and Public Papers of John Jay*, Vol. 4, p. 484.]

11. *The Christian religion when divested of the rags in which they have enveloped it, and brought to the original purity and simplicity of its benevolent institutor, is a religion of all others most friendly to liberty.* —THOMAS JEFFERSON

[To Moses Robinson. Adams, *Jefferson's Extracts*, p. 325.]

12. *God who gave us life gave us liberty. And can the liberties of a nation be thought secure when we have removed their only firm basis, a conviction in the minds of the people that these liberties are of the Gift of God? That they are not to be violated but with his wrath? Indeed, I tremble for my country when I reflect that God is just; that His justice cannot sleep forever.* —THOMAS JEFFERSON

[Thomas Jefferson, *Notes on Virginia*, Query XVIII, 1781, 1782, p. 237.]

13. *Religion is the basis and Foundation of Government.* —JAMES MADISON

[Robert Rutland, ed., *The Papers of James Madison*, Vol. VIII (Chicago: University of Chicago Press, 1973), pp. 299, 304.]

14. *The belief in a God All Powerful wise and good, is . . . essential to the moral order of the World and to the happiness of man.* —JAMES MADISON

[Letter to Frederick Beasley, November 20, 1825.]

15. *It is the duty of every man to render to the Creator such homage. . . . Before any man can be considered as a member of Civil Society, he must be considered as a subject of the Governor of the Universe.* —JAMES MADISON

[James Madison, *A Memorial and Remonstrance* (Washington DC: Library of Congress, Rare Book Collection, delivered to the General Assembly of the State of Virginia, 1785).]

16. *The American population is entirely Christian, and with us Christianity and Religion are identified. It would be strange indeed, if with such a people, our institutions did not presuppose Christianity, and did not often refer to it, and exhibit relations with it.* —JOHN MARSHALL

[Letter to Jasper Adams, May 9, 1833, *James McClellan, Joseph Story and the American Constitution* (Norman, OK: University of Oklahoma, 1971), p. 139.]

17. *It is foreign to my purpose to hint at the arguments which establish the truth of Christian revelation. My only business is to declare, that all its doctrines and precepts are calculated to promote the happiness of society, and the safety and well being of civil government.* —BENJAMIN RUSH

[Benjamin Rush, "Of the Mode of Education Proper in a Republic," in *Essays: Literary, Moral and Philosophical*, p. 6.]

18. *I have always considered Christianity as the strong ground of republicanism. The spirit is opposed, not only to the splendor, but even to the very forms of monarchy, and many of its precepts have for their objects republican liberty and equality as well as simplicity, integrity, and economy in government. It is only necessary for republicanism to ally itself to the Christian religion to overturn all the corrupted political and religious institutions in the world.* —BENJAMIN RUSH

[To Thomas Jefferson, August 22, 1800, Butterfield, Letters of Rush, 2:820–21.]

19. *True religion affords to government its surest support.* —GEORGE WASHINGTON

[To the Synod of the Reformed Dutch Church of North America, October 1789, Washington Papers, Library of Congress.]

20. *Religion and Morality are the essential pillars of Civil society.* —GEORGE WASHINGTON

[Letter to the Clergy of Different Denominations Residing in and near the City of Philadelphia, March 3, 1797.]

APPENDIX 2

WORDS FROM THE FRONTLINES OF FAITH

One of the most difficult tasks for an historian is to convince readers that the words of people who lived history are usually more thrilling than the words of people who describe history. Like finding a great-grandmother's letters in the attic, there is more personality and adventure, greater simplicity and emotion, in the original documents.

C. S. Lewis explained this well in his introduction to Athanasius's work on the Incarnation.

> There is a strange idea abroad that in every subject the ancient books should be read only by the professionals, and that the amateur should content himself with the modern books. Thus I have found as a tutor in English Literature that if the average student wants to find out something about Platonism, the very last thing he thinks of doing is to take a translation of Plato off the library shelf and read the Symposium. He would rather read some dreary modern book ten times as long, all about "isms" and influences and only once in twelve pages telling him what Plato actually said. The error is rather an amiable one, for it springs from humility. The student is half afraid to meet one of the great philosophers face to face. He feels himself inadequate and thinks he will not understand him. But if he only knew, the great man, just because of his greatness, is much more intelligible than his modern commentator. The simplest student will be able to understand, if not all, yet a very great deal of what Plato said; but hardly anyone can understand some modern books on Platonism. It has always therefore been one of my main endeavors as a teacher to persuade the young that first-hand knowledge is not only more worth acquiring than secondhand knowledge, but is usually much easier and more delightful to acquire.

This is certainly true of the original writings of American history. Since ours is a relatively recent history, since many of the nation's greatest figures were also gifted writers, and since Americans have felt the need to declare themselves to the watching world more than most other cultures, our nation's past is filled with easily accessible literary drama.

Some of that drama is presented here. Sadly, it is of the type that most readers miss. Few nonlawyers would dare to read a Supreme Court ruling or assume that they could understand the statutes of a state dating from the 1700s. Hopefully, what follows will lead to a different view of how thrilling such documents—understood in their historical setting—can be.

Presented below, then, is the full text of some of the most important documents relating to religion in American public life.

1. Justice Hugo Black's Majority Opinion in *Everson v. Board of Education*
2. James Madison's "Memorial and Remonstrance"
3. James Madison's "Detached Memorandum"
4. Thomas Jefferson's Five Bills on Religion in the Virginia Statutes
5. Justice William Rehnquist's Dissent in *Wallace v. Jaffree*

Though each of these documents has already been described in the text of this book, there is still a brief paragraph of introduction provided here as a reminder. The text of the Danbury Baptist Association's letter to Jefferson and his historic response would naturally be included here, but they have already been provided in their entirety in chapter 2. To make the Black and Rehnquist documents more readable, all citations and legal notations have been removed in the belief that the average reader doesn't need them and those who do need them know where to find them.

JUSTICE HUGO BLACK'S MAJORITY OPINION IN EVERSON V. BOARD OF EDUCATION

It was in the Everson case of 1947 that the Supreme Court issued its historic ruling that the Establishment Clause erected a "wall of separation between church and state." This was the first time that Jefferson's phrase from the Danbury letter took on the force of law. Hugo Black wrote the majority opinion in the case, certainly one of the most controversial in the Court's long history.

A New Jersey statute authorizes its local school districts to make rules and contracts for the transportation of children to and from schools. The appellee, a township board of education, acting pursuant to this statute authorized reimbursement to parents of money expended by them for the bus transportation of their children on regular busses operated by the public transportation system. Part of this money was for the payment of transportation of some children in the community to Catholic parochial schools. These church schools give their students, in addition to secular education, regular religious instruction conforming to the religious tenets and modes of worship of the Catholic Faith. The superintendent of these schools is a Catholic priest.

The appellant, in his capacity as a district taxpayer, filed suit in a State court challenging the right of the Board to reimburse parents of parochial school students. He contended that the statute and the resolution passed pursuant to it violated both the State and the Federal Constitutions. That court held that the legislature was without power to authorize such payment under the State constitution. The New Jersey Court of Errors and Appeals reversed, holding that neither the statute nor the resolution passed pursuant to it was in conflict with the State constitution or the provisions of the Federal Constitution in issue.

Since there has been no attack on the statute on the ground that a part of its language excludes children attending private schools operated for profit from enjoying state payment for their transportation, we need not consider this exclusionary language; it has no relevancy to any constitutional question here presented. Furthermore, if the exclusion clause had been properly challenged, we do not know whether New Jersey's highest court would construe its statutes as precluding payment of the school transportation of any group of pupils, even those of a private school run for profit. Consequently, we put to one side the question as to the validity of the statute against the claim that it does not authorize payment for the transportation generally of school children in New Jersey.

The only contention here is that the State statute and the resolution, in so far as they authorized reimbursement to parents of children attending parochial schools, violate the Federal Constitution in these two respects, which to some extent, overlap. First. They authorize the State to take by taxation the private property of some and bestow it upon others, to be used for their own private purposes. This, it is alleged violates the due process clause of the Fourteenth Amendment. Second. The statute and the resolution forced inhabitants to pay taxes to help support and maintain schools which are dedicated to, and which regularly teach, the Catholic Faith. This is alleged to be a use of State power to support church schools contrary to the prohibition of the First Amendment which the Fourteenth Amendment made applicable to the states.

First. The due process argument that the State law taxes some people to help others carry out their private purposes is framed in two phases. The first phase is that a state cannot tax A to reimburse B for the cost of transporting his children to church schools. This is said to violate the due process clause because the children are sent to these church schools to satisfy the personal desires of their parents, rather than the public's interest in the general education of all children. This argument, if valid, would apply equally to prohibit state payment for the transportation of children to any non-public school, whether operated by a church, or any other non-government individual or group. But, the New Jersey legislature has decided that a public purpose will be served by using tax-raised funds to pay the bus fares of all school children, including those who attend parochial schools. The New Jersey Court of Errors and Appeals has reached the same conclusion. The fact that a state law, passed to satisfy a public need, coincides with the personal desires of the individuals most directly affected is certainly an inadequate reason for us to say that a legislature has erroneously appraised the public need.

It is true that this Court has, in rare instances, struck down state statutes on the ground that the purpose for which tax-raised funds were to be expended was not a public one. But the Court has also pointed out that this far-reaching authority must be exercised with the most extreme caution. Otherwise, a state's power to legislate for the public welfare might be seriously curtailed, a power which is a primary reason for the existence of states. Changing local conditions create new local problems which may lead a state's people and its local authorities to believe that laws authorizing new types of public services are necessary to promote the general well-being of the people. The Fourteenth Amendment did not strip the states of their power to meet problems previously left for individual solution.

It is much too late to argue that legislation intended to facilitate the opportunity of children to get a secular education serves no public purpose. The same thing is no less true of legislation to reimburse needy parents, or all parents, for payment of the fares of their children so that they can ride in public buses to and from schools rather than run the risk of traffic and other hazards incident to walking or hitchhiking. Nor does it follow that a law has a private rather than a public purpose because it provides that tax-raised funds will be paid to reimburse individuals on account of money spent by them in a way which furthers a public program. Subsidies and loans to individuals such as farmers and home owners, and to privately owned transportation systems, as well as many other kinds of businesses, have been commonplace practices in our state and national history.

Insofar as the second phase of the due process argument may differ from the first, it is by suggesting that taxation for transportation of children to church schools constitutes support of a religion by the State. But if the law is invalid for this reason, it is because it violates the First Amendment's prohibition against the establishment of religion by law. This is the exact question raised by appellant's second contention, to consideration of which we now turn.

Second. The New Jersey statute is challenged as a "law respecting an establishment of religion." The First Amendment, as made applicable to the states by the Fourteenth, commands that a state "shall make no law respecting an establishment of religion, or prohibiting the free exercise thereof." These words of the First Amendment reflected in the minds of early Americans a vivid mental picture of conditions and practices which they fervently wished to stamp out in order to preserve liberty for themselves and for their posterity. Doubtless their goal has not been entirely reached; but so far has the Nation moved toward it that the expression "law respecting an establishment of religion," probably does not so vividly remind present-day Americans of the evils, fears, and political problems that caused that expression to be written into our Bill of Rights. Whether this New Jersey law is one respecting the "establishment of religion" requires an understanding of the meaning of that language, particularly with respect to the imposition of taxes. Once again, therefore, it is not inappropriate briefly to review the background and environment of the period in which that constitutional language was fashioned and adopted.

A large proportion of the early settlers of this country came here from Europe to escape the bondage of laws which compelled them to support and attend government favored churches. The centuries immediately before and contemporaneous with the colonization of America had been filled with turmoil, civil strife, and persecutions, generated in large part by established sects determined to maintain their absolute political and religious supremacy. With the power of government supporting them, at various times and places, Catholics had persecuted Protestants, Protestants had persecuted Catholics, Protestant sects had persecuted other Protestant sects, Catholics of one shade of belief had persecuted Catholics of another shade of belief, and all of these had from time to time persecuted Jews. In efforts to force loyalty to whatever religious group happened to be on top and in league with the government of a particular time and place, men and women had been fined, cast in jail, cruelly tortured, and killed. Among the offenses for which these punishments had been inflicted were such things as speaking disrespectfully of the views of ministers of government-established churches, nonattendance at those churches, expressions of non-belief in their doctrines, and failure to pay taxes and tithes to support them.

These practices of the old world were transplanted to and began to thrive in the soil of the new America. The very charters granted by the English Crown to the individuals and companies designated to make the laws which would control the destinies of the colonials authorized these individuals and companies to erect religious establishments which all, whether believers or non-believers, would be required to support and attend. An exercise of this authority was accompanied by a repetition of many of the old world practices and persecutions. Catholics found themselves hounded and proscribed because of their faith; Quakers who followed their conscience went to jail; Baptists were peculiarly obnoxious to certain dominant Protestant sects; men and women of varied faiths who happened to be in a minority in a particular locality were persecuted because they steadfastly persisted in worshipping God only as their own consciences dictated. And all of these dissenters were compelled to pay tithes and taxes to support government-sponsored churches whose ministers preached inflammatory sermons designed to strengthen and consolidate the established faith by generating a burning hatred against dissenters. These practices became so commonplace as to shock the freedom-loving colonials into a feeling of abhorrence. The imposition of taxes to pay ministers' salaries and to build and maintain churches and church property aroused their indignation. It was these feelings which found expression in the First Amendment. No one locality and no one group throughout the Colonies can rightly be given entire credit for having aroused the sentiment that culminated in adoption of the Bill of Rights' provisions embracing religious liberty. But Virginia, where the established church had achieved a dominant influence in political affairs and where many excesses attracted wide public attention, provided a great stimulus and able leadership for the movement. The people there, as elsewhere, reached the conviction that individual religious liberty could be achieved best under a government which was stripped of all power to tax, to support, or otherwise to assist any or all religions, or to interfere with the beliefs of any religious individual or group.

The movement toward this end reached its dramatic climax in Virginia in 1785-86 when the Virginia legislative body was about to renew Virginia's tax levy for the support of the established church. Thomas Jefferson and James Madison led the fight against this tax. Madison wrote his great Memorial and Remonstrance against the law. In it, he eloquently argued that a true religion did not need the support of law; that no person, either believer or non-believer, should be taxed to support a religious institution of any kind; that the best interest of a society required that the minds of men always be wholly free; and that cruel persecutions were the inevitable result of government-established religions. Madison's Remonstrance received strong support throughout Virginia, and the Assembly postponed consideration of the proposed tax measure until its next session. When the proposal came up for consideration at that session, it not only died in committee, but the Assembly enacted the famous "Virginia Bill for Religious Liberty" originally written by Thomas Jefferson. The preamble to that Bill stated among other things that

Almighty God hath created the mind free; that all attempts to influence it by temporal punishments, or burthens [burdens], or by civil incapacitations, tend only to beget habits of hypocrisy and meanness, and are a departure from the plan of the Holy author of our religion who being Lord both of body and mind, yet chose not to propagate it by coercions on either; that to compel a man to furnish contributions of money for the propagation of opinions which he disbelieves, is sinful and tyrannical; that even the forcing him to support this or that teacher of his own religious persuasion, is depriving him of the comfortable liberty of giving his contributions to the particular pastor, whose morals he would make his pattern . . .

And the statute itself enacted

That no man shall be compelled to frequent or support any religious worship, place, or ministry whatsoever, nor shall be enforced, restrained, molested, or burdened, in his body or goods, nor shall otherwise suffer on account of his religious opinions or belief . . .

This Court has previously recognized that the provisions of the First Amendment, in the drafting and adoption of which Madison and

Jefferson played such leading roles, had the same objective and were intended to provide the same protection against governmental intrusion on religious liberty as the Virginia statute. Prior to the adoption of the Fourteenth Amendment, the First Amendment did not apply as a restraint against the states. Most of them did soon provide similar constitutional protections for religious liberty. But some states persisted for about half a century in imposing restraints upon the free exercise of religion and in discriminating against particular religious groups. In recent years, so far as the provision against the establishment of a religion is concerned, the question has most frequently arisen in connection with proposed state aid to church schools and efforts to carry on religious teachings in the public schools in accordance with the tenets of a particular sect. Some churches have either sought or accepted state financial support for their schools. Here again the efforts to obtain state aid or acceptance of it have not been limited to any one particular faith. The state courts, in the main, have remained faithful to the language of their own constitutional provisions designed to protect religious freedom and to separate religions and governments. Their decisions, however, show the difficulty in drawing the line between tax legislation which provides funds for the welfare of the general public and that which is designed to support institutions which teach religion.

The meaning and scope of the First Amendment, preventing establishment of religion or prohibiting the free exercise thereof, in the light of its history and the evils it was designed forever to suppress, have been several times elaborated by the decisions of this Court prior to the application of the First Amendment to the states by the Fourteenth. The broad meaning given the Amendment by these earlier cases has been accepted by this Court in its decisions concerning an individual's religious freedom rendered since the Fourteenth Amendment was interpreted to make the prohibitions of the First applicable to state action abridging religious freedom. There is every reason to give the same application and broad interpretation to the "establishment of religion" clause. The interrelation of these complementary clauses was well summarized in a statement of the Court of Appeals of South Carolina: "The structure of our government has, for the preservation of civil liberty, rescued the temporal institutions from religious inter-ference. On the other hand, it has secured religious liberty from the invasions of the civil authority."

The "establishment of religion" clause of the First Amendment means at least this: Neither a state nor the Federal Government can set up a church. Neither can pass laws which aid one religion, aid all reli-gions, or prefer one religion over another. Neither can force nor influ-ence a person to go to or to remain away from church against his will or force him to profess a belief or disbelief in any religion. No person can be punished for entertaining or professing religious beliefs or dis-beliefs, for church attendance or non-attendance. No tax in any amount, large or small, can be levied to support any religious activi-ties or institutions, whatever they may be called, or whatever form they may adopt to teach or practice religion. Neither a state nor the Federal Government can, openly or secretly, participate in the affairs of any religious organizations or groups and vice versa. In the words of Jefferson, the clause against establishment of religion by law was intended to erect "a wall of separation between Church and State."

We must consider the New Jersey statute in accordance with the foregoing limitations imposed by the First Amendment. But we must not strike that state statute down if it is within the state's constitu-tional power even though it approaches the verge of that power. New Jersey cannot consistently with the "establishment of religion" clause of the First Amendment contribute tax-raised funds to the support of an institution which teaches the tenets and faith of any church. On the other hand, other language of the amendment commands that New Jersey cannot hamper its citizens in the free exercise of their own religion. Consequently, it cannot exclude individual Catholics, Lutherans, Mohammedans, Baptists, Jews, Methodists, Non-believers, Presbyterians, or the members of any other faith, because of their faith, or lack of it, from receiving the benefits of public welfare legislation. While we do not mean to intimate that a state could not provide transportation only to children attending public schools, we must be careful, in protecting the citizens of New Jersey against state-established churches, to be sure that we do not inadvertently prohibit New Jersey from extending its general State law benefits to all its citizens without regard to their religious belief. Measured by these standards, we cannot say that the First Amendment prohibits New Jersey from spending tax-raised funds to pay the bus fares of parochial school pupils as a part of a general program under which it pays the fares of pupils attending public and other schools. It is undoubtedly true that children are helped to get to church schools. There is even a possibility that some of the children might not be sent to the church schools if the parents were compelled to pay their children's bus fares out of their own pockets when transportation to a public school would have been paid for by the State. The same possibility exists where the state requires a local transit company to provide reduced fares to school children including those attending parochial schools, or where a municipally owned transportation system undertakes to carry all school children free of charge. Moreover, state-paid policemen, detailed to protect children going to and from church schools from the very real hazards of traffic, would serve much the same purpose and accomplish much the same result as state provisions intended to guarantee free transportation of a kind which the state deems to be best for the school children's welfare. And parents might refuse to risk their children to the serious danger of traffic accidents going to and from parochial schools, the approaches to which were not protected by policemen. Similarly, parents might be reluctant to permit their children to attend schools which the state had cut off from such general government services as ordinary police and fire protection, connections for sewage disposal, public highways and sidewalks. Of course, cutting off church schools from these services, so separate and so indisputably marked off from the religious function, would make it far more difficult for the schools to operate. But such is obviously not the purpose of the First Amendment. That Amendment requires the state to be a neutral in its relations with groups of religious believers and non-believers; it does not require the state to be their adversary. State power is no more to be used so as to handicap religions, than it is to favor them.

This Court has said that parents may, in the discharge of their duty under state compulsory education laws, send their children to a religious rather than a public school if the school meets the secular educational requirements which the state has power to impose. It appears that these parochial schools meet New Jersey's requirements. The State contributes no money to the schools. It does not support them. Its legislation, as applied, does no more than provide a general program to help parents get their children, regardless of their religion, safely and expeditiously to and from accredited schools.

The First Amendment has erected a wall between church and state. That wall must be kept high and impregnable. We could not approve the slightest breach. New Jersey has not breached it here.

JAMES MADISON'S "MEMORIAL AND REMONSTRANCE"

James Madison wrote his "Memorial and Remonstrance" in 1785 to oppose a Virginia bill entitled "A Bill Establishing a Provision of Teachers of the Christian Religion." Justice Black relied upon Madison's "Memorial" in interpreting the original intent of the First Amendment, and the document has become one of the most often cited sources for understanding the religious views of the founding fathers.

To The General Assembly of the Commonwealth of Virginia
A Memorial and Remonstrance
By James Madison, 1785

We the subscribers, citizens of the said commonwealth, having taken into serious consideration a bill printed by order of the last session of general assembly, entitled "A Bill establishing a provision for Teachers of the Christian Religion," and conceiving that the same if finally armed with the sanctions of a law, will be a dangerous abuse of power, are bound as faithful members of a free state to remonstrate against it, and to declare the reasons by which we are determined. We remonstrate against the said bill,

1. Because we hold it for a fundamental and undeniable truth, "that religion or the duty which we owe to our Creator and the manner of discharging it can be directed only by reason and conviction, not by force or violence." The religion then of every man must be left to the conviction and conscience of every man; and it is the right of every man to exercise it as these may dictate. This right is in its nature an unalienable right. It is unalienable, because the opinions

of men, depending only on the evidence contemplated by their own minds cannot follow the dictates of other men: It is unalienable also, because what is here a right towards men is a duty towards the Creator. It is the duty of every man to render to the Creator such homage and such only as he believes to be acceptable to him. This duty is precedent, both in order of time and in degree of obligation, to the claims of civil society. Before any man can be considered as a member of civil society, he must be considered as a subject of the Governor of the Universe: And if a member of civil society, do it with a saving of his allegiance to the Universal Sovereign. We maintain therefore that in matters of religion, no man's right is abridged by the institution of civil society and that religion is wholly exempt from its cognizance. True it is, that no other rule exists, by which any question which may divide a society, can be ultimately determined, but the will of the majority; but it is also true that the majority may trespass on the rights of the minority.

2. Because religion be exempt from the authority of the society at large, still less can it be subject to that of the legislative body. The latter are but the creatures and vicegerents of the former. Their jurisdiction is both derivative and limited: it is limited with regard to the coordinate departments, more necessarily is it limited with regard to the constituents. The preservation of a free government requires not merely, that the metes and bounds which separate each department of power be invariably maintained; but more especially that neither of them be suffered to overleap the great barrier which defends the rights of the people. The rulers who are guilty of such an encroachment, exceed the commission from which they derive their authority, and are tyrants. The people who submit to it are governed by laws made neither by themselves nor by an authority derived from them, and are slaves.

3. Because it is proper to take alarm at the first experiment on our liberties. We hold this prudent jealousy to be the first duty of citizens, and one of the noblest characteristics of the late Revolution. The free men of America did not wait till usurped power had strengthened itself by exercise, and entangled the question in precedents. They saw all the consequences in the principle, and they avoided the consequences by denying the principle. We revere this lesson too much soon to forget it. Who does not see that the same authority which can establish Christianity, in exclusion of all other religions, may establish with the same ease any particular sect of Christians, in exclusion of all other sects? That the same authority which can force a citizen to contribute three pence only of his property for the support of any one establishment, may force him to conform to any other establishment in all cases whatsoever?

4. Because the bill violates the equality which ought to be the basis of every law, and which is more indispensable, in proportion as the validity or expediency of any law is more liable to be impeached. If "all men are by nature equally free and independent," all men are to be considered as entering into society on equal conditions; as relinquishing no more, and therefore retaining no less, one than another, of their natural rights. Above all are they to be considered as retaining an "equal title to the free exercise of religion according to the dictates of conscience." While we assert for ourselves a freedom to embrace, to profess and to observe the religion which we believe to be of divine origin, we cannot deny an equal freedom to those whose minds have not yet yielded to the evidence which has convinced us. If this freedom be abused, it is an offense against God, not against man: To God, therefore, not to man, must an account of it be rendered. As the bill violates equality by subjecting some to peculiar burdens, so it violates the

same principle, by granting to others peculiar exemptions. Are the Quakers and Menonists [Mennonites] the only sects who think a compulsive support of their religions unnecessary and unwarrantable? Can their piety alone be entrusted with the care of public worship? Ought their religions to be endowed above all others with extraordinary privileges by which proselytes may be enticed from all others? We think too favorably of the justice and good sense of these denominations to believe that they either covet pre-eminences over their fellow citizens or that they will be seduced by them from the common opposition to the measure.

5. Because the bill implies either that the civil magistrate is a competent judge of religious truth; or that he may employ religion as an engine of civil policy. The first is an arrogant pretension falsified by the contradictory opinions of rulers in all ages, and throughout the world: the second an unhallowed perversion of the means of salvation.

6. Because the establishment proposed by the bill is not requisite for the support of the Christian religion. To say that it is, is a contradiction to the Christian religion itself, for every page of it disavows a dependence on the powers of this world: it is a contradiction to fact; for it is known that this religion both existed and flourished, not only without the support of human laws, but in spite of every opposition from them, and not only during the period of miraculous aid, but long after it had been left to its own evidence and the ordinary care of Providence. Nay, it is a contradiction in terms; for a religion not invented by human policy, must have pre-existed and been supported, before it was established by human policy. It is moreover to weaken in those who profess this religion a pious confidence in its innate excellence and the patronage of its author;

and to foster in those who still reject it, a suspicion that its friends are too conscious of its fallacies to trust it to its own merits.

7. Because experience witnesses that ecclesiastical establishments, instead of maintaining the purity and efficacy of religion, have had a contrary operation. During almost fifteen centuries has the legal establishment of Christianity been on trial. What have been its fruits? More or less in all places, pride and indolence in the clergy, ignorance and servility in the laity, in both, superstition, bigotry and persecution. Inquire of the teachers of Christianity for the ages in which it appeared in its greatest luster; those of every sect, point to the ages prior to its incorporation with civil policy. Propose a restoration of this primitive state in which its teachers depended on the voluntary rewards of their flocks, many of them predict its downfall. On which side ought their testimony to have greatest weight, when for or when against their interest?

8. Because the establishment in question is not necessary for the support of civil government. If it be urged as necessary for the support of civil government only as it is a means of supporting religion, and it be not necessary for the latter purpose, it cannot be necessary for the former. If religion be not within the cognizance of civil government how can its legal establishment be necessary to civil government? What influence in fact have ecclesiastical establishments had on civil society? In some instances they have been seen to erect a spiritual tyranny on the ruins of the civil authority; in many instances they have been seen upholding the thrones of political tyranny: in no instance have they been seen the guardians of the liberties of the people. Rulers who wished to subvert the public liberty, may have found an established clergy convenient auxiliaries. A just government instituted

to secure and perpetuate it needs them not. Such a government will be best supported by protecting every citizen in the enjoyment of his religion with the same equal hand which protects his person and his property; by neither invading the equal rights of any sect, nor suffering any sect to invade those of another.

9. Because the proposed establishment is a departure from the generous policy, which, offering an asylum to the persecuted and oppressed of every nation and religion, promised a luster to our country, and an accession to the number of its citizens. What a melancholy mark is the bill of sudden degeneracy? Instead of holding forth an asylum to the persecuted, it is itself a signal of persecution. It degrades from the equal rank of citizens all those whose opinions in religion do not bend to those of the legislative authority. Distant as it may be in its present form from the Inquisition, it differs from it only in degree. The one is the first step, the other the last in the career of intolerance. The magnanimous sufferer under this cruel scourge in foreign regions, must view the bill as a beacon on our coast, warning him to seek some other haven, where liberty and philanthropy in their due extent, may offer a more certain repose from his troubles.

10. Because it will have a like tendency to banish our citizens. The allurements presented by other situations are every day thinning their number. To superadd a fresh motive to emigration by revoking the liberty which they now enjoy, would be the same species of folly which has dishonored and depopulated flourishing kingdoms.

11. Because it will destroy that moderation and harmony which the forbearance of our laws to intermeddle with religion has produced among its several sects. Torrents of blood have been spilt in the old

world, by vain attempts of the secular arm, to extinguish religious discord, by proscribing all difference in religious opinion. Time has at length revealed the true remedy. Every relaxation of narrow and rigorous policy, wherever it has been tried, has been found to assuage the disease. The American theatre has exhibited proofs that equal and complete liberty, if it does not wholly eradicate it, sufficiently destroys its malignant influence on the health and prosperity of the state. If with the salutary effects of this system under our own eyes, we begin to contract the bounds of religious freedom, we know no name that will too severely reproach our folly. At least let warning be taken at the first fruits of the threatened innovation. The very appearance of the bill has transformed "that Christian forbearance, love and charity," which of late mutually prevailed, into animosities and jealousies, which may not soon be appeased. What mischief may not be dreaded, should this enemy to the public quiet be armed with the force of a law?

12. Because the policy of the bill is adverse to the diffusion of the light of Christianity. The first wish of those who enjoy this precious gift ought to be that it may be imparted to the whole race of mankind. Compare the number of those who have as yet received it with the number still remaining under the dominion of false religions; and how small is the former! Does the policy of the bill tend to lessen the disproportion? No; it at once discourages those who are strangers to the light of revelation from coming into the region of it; and countenances by example the nations who continue in darkness, in shutting out those who might convey it to them. Instead of leveling as far as possible, every obstacle to the victorious progress of truth, the bill with an ignoble and unchristian timidity would circumscribe it with a wall of defense against the encroachments of error.

13. Because attempts to enforce by legal sanctions, acts obnoxious to so great a proportion of citizens, tend to enervate the laws in general, and to slacken the bands of society. If it be difficult to execute any law which is not generally deemed necessary or salutary, what must be the case, where it is deemed invalid and dangerous? And what may be the effect of so striking an example of impotency in the government, on its general authority?

14. Because a measure of such singular magnitude and delicacy ought not to be imposed, without the clearest evidence that it is called for by a majority of citizens, and no satisfactory method is yet proposed by which the voice of the majority in this case may be determined, or its influence secured. The people of the respective counties are indeed requested to signify their opinion respecting the adoption of the bill to the next session of assembly. But the representatives of the counties will be that of the people. Our hope is that neither of the former will, after due consideration, espouse the dangerous principle of the bill. Should the event disappoint us, it will still leave us in full confidence, that a fair appeal to the latter will reverse the sentence against our liberties.

15. Because finally, "the equal right of every citizen to the free exercise of his religion according to the dictates of conscience" is held by the same tenure with all our other rights. If we recur to its origin, it is equally the gift of nature; if we weigh its importance, it cannot be less dear to us; if we consult the "Declaration of those rights which pertain to the good people of Virginia, as the basis and foundation of Government," it is enumerated with equal solemnity, or rather studied emphasis. Either we must say, that the will of the legislature is the only measure of their authority; and that in the plenitude of this authority, they may sweep away all

our fundamental rights; or, that they are bound to leave this particular right untouched and sacred: Either we must say, that they may control the freedom of the press, may abolish the trial by jury, may swallow up the executive and judiciary powers of the state; nay that they may despoil us of our very right of suffrage, and erect themselves into an independent and hereditary assembly or, we must say, that they have no authority to enact into the law the bill under consideration. We the subscribers say, that the general assembly of this commonwealth have no such authority: and that no effort may be omitted on our part against so dangerous an usurpation, we oppose to it, this remonstrance; earnestly praying, as we are in duty bound, that the Supreme Lawgiver of the Universe, by illuminating those to whom it is addressed, may on the one hand, turn their councils from every act which would affront his holy prerogative, or violate the trust committed to them: and on the other, guide them into every measure which may be worthy of his blessing, may redound to their own praise, and may establish more firmly the liberties, the prosperity and the happiness of the commonwealth.

JAMES MADISON'S "DETACHED MEMORANDUM"

James Madison wrote his "Detached Memorandum" long after he had retired from public life and possibly as late as 1823. The document was largely unknown until 1946 when it was discovered in a box of unrelated papers and published in the *William and Mary Quarterly*. The "Detached Memorandum" was cited by Justice Black in the *Everson* case and continues to be influential in the American separation-of-church-and-state debate.

> The danger of silent accumulations and encroachments by ecclesiastical bodies have not sufficiently engaged attention in the U.S. They have the noble merit of first unshackling the conscience from persecuting laws, and of establishing among religious seas a legal equality. If some of the States have not embraced this just and this truly Christian principle in its proper latitude, all of them present examples by which the most enlightened states of the old world may be instructed; and there is one state at least, Virginia, where religious liberty is placed on its true foundation and is defined in its full latitude. The general principle is contained in her declaration of rights, prefixed to her constitution, but it is unfolded and defined in its precise extent in the act of the legislature, usually named the Religious Bill, which passed into a law in the year 1786. Here the separation between the authority of human laws and the natural rights of man excepted from the grant on which all political authority is founded is traced as distinctly as words can admit, and the limits to this authority established with as much solemnity as the forms of legislation can express.
>
> The law has the further advantage of having been the result of a formal appeal to the sense of the community and a deliberate sanction of a vast majority comprising every sect of Christians in the State. This

act is a true standard of religious liberty: its principle the great barrier against usurpations on the rights of conscience. As long as it is respected and no longer, these will be safe. Every provision for them short of this principle will be found to leave crevices at least through which bigotry may introduce persecution; a monster, that feeding and thriving on its own venom, gradually swells to a size and strength overwhelming all laws divine and human.

You States of America, which retain in your constitutions or codes any aberration from the sacred principle of religious liberty, by giving to Caesar what belongs to God, or joining together what God has put asunder, hasten to revise and purify your systems and make the example of your country as pure and complete in what relates to the freedom of the mind and its allegiance to its maker, as in what belongs to the legitimate objects of political and civil institutions.

Strongly guarded as is the separation between religion and government in the Constitution of the United States the danger of encroachment by ecclesiastical bodies may be illustrated by precedents already furnished in their short history.

The most notable attempt was that in Virginia to establish a general assessment for the support of all Christian sects. This was proposed in the year 1784 by Patrick Henry and supported by all his eloquence, aided by the remaining prejudices of the sect which before the Revolution had been established by law. The progress of the measure was arrested by urging that the respect due to the people required in so extraordinary a case an appeal to their deliberate will. The bill was accordingly printed and published with that view. At the insistence of Colonel George Nicholas, Colonel George Mason and others, the memorial and remonstrance against it was drawn up, and printed copies of it circulated through the State to be signed by the people at large. It met with the approbation of the Baptists, the Presbyterians, the Quakers, and the few Roman Catholics, universally; of the

Methodists in part; and even of not a few of the sect formerly established by law. When the legislature assembled, the number of copies and signatures prescribed displayed such an overwhelming opposition of the people that the proposed plan of a general assessment was crushed under it and advantage taken of the crisis to carry through the legislature the bill above referred to establishing religious liberty.

In the course of the opposition to the bill in the House of Delegates, which was warm and strenuous from some of the minority, an experiment was made on the reverence entertained for the name and sanctity of the Savior by proposing to insert the words "Jesus Christ" after the words "our lord" in the preamble, the object of which would have been to imply a restriction of the liberty defined in the bill to those professing his religion only. The amendment was discussed and rejected by a vote of against. The opponents of the amendment having turned the feeling as well as judgment of the House against it, by successfully contending that the better proof of reverence for that holy name would be not to profane it by making it a topic of legislative discussion, and particularly by making his religion the means of abridging the natural and equal rights of all men, in defiance of his own declaration that his kingdom was not of this world. This view of the subject was much enforced by the circumstance that it was espoused by some members who were particularly distinguished by their reputed piety and Christian zeal.

But besides the danger of a direct mixture of religion and civil government, there is an evil which ought to be guarded against in the indefinite accumulation of property from the capacity of holding it in perpetuity by ecclesiastical corporations. The power of all corporations ought to be limited in this respect. The growing wealth acquired by them never fails to be a source of abuses. A warning on this subject is emphatically given in the example of the various charitable establishments in Great Britain the management of which has been lately scrutinized. The excessive wealth of ecclesiastical corporations and the misuse of it in many countries of Europe has long been a topic of complaint. In some of them the Church has amassed half perhaps the property of the nation. When the reformation took place, an event promoted if not caused by that disordered state of things, how enormous were the treasures of religious societies, and how gross the corruptions engendered by them; so enormous and so gross as to produce in the cabinets and councils of the protestant States a disregard of all the pleas of the interested party drawn from the sanctions of the law, and the sacredness of property held in religious trust. The history of England during the period of the reformation offers a sufficient illustration for the present purpose.

Are the U.S. duly awake to the tendency of the precedents they are establishing, in the multiplied incorporations of religious congregations with the faculty of acquiring and holding property real as well as personal! Do not many of these acts give this faculty, without limit either as to time or as to amount! And must not bodies, perpetual in their existence, and which may be always gaining without ever losing, speedily gain more than is useful, and in time more than is safe! Are there not already examples in the U.S. of ecclesiastical wealth equally beyond its object and the foresight of those who laid the foundation of it! In the U.S. there is a double motive for fixing limits in this case, because wealth may increase not only from additional gifts, but from exorbitant advances in the value of the primitive one. In grants of vacant lands, and of lands in the vicinity of growing towns and cities the increase of value is often such as if foreseen, would essentially control the liberality confirming them. The people of the U.S. owe their independence and their liberty, to the wisdom of descrying in the minute tax of three pence on tea, the magnitude of the evil comprised in the precedent. Let them exert the same wisdom, in watching against every evil lurking under plausible disguises, and growing up from small beginnings. Obsta principiis [Resist the beginnings].

Is the appointment of chaplains to the two houses of Congress consistent with the Constitution, and with the pure principle of religious freedom? In strictness the answer on both points must be in the negative. The Constitution of the U.S. forbids everything like an establishment of a national religion. The law appointing chaplains establishes a religious worship for the national representatives, to be performed by ministers of religion, elected by a majority of them; and these are to be paid out of the national taxes. Does not this involve the principle of a national establishment, applicable to a provision for a religious worship for the constituent as well as of the representative body, approved by the majority, and conducted by ministers of religion paid by the entire nation?

The establishment of the chaplain to Congress is a palpable violation of equal rights, as well as of Constitutional principles. The tenets of the chaplains elected by the majority shut the door of worship against the members whose creeds and consciences forbid a participation in that of the majority. To say nothing of other sects, this is the case with that of Roman Catholics and Quakers who have always had members in one or both of the legislative branches. Could a Catholic clergyman ever hope to be appointed a chaplain! To say that his religious principles are obnoxious or that his sect is small is to lift the evil at once and exhibit in its naked deformity the doctrine that religious truth is to be tested by numbers or that the major sects have a right to govern the minor.

If religion consist in voluntary acts of individuals, singly, or voluntarily associated, and it be proper that public functionaries, as well as their constituents should discharge their religious duties, let them like their constituents do so at their own expense. How small a contribution from each member of Congress would suffice for the purpose! How just would it be in its principle! How noble in its exemplary sacrifice to the genius of the Constitution; and the divine right of conscience! Why should the expense of a religious worship be allowed for the legislature, be paid by the public, more than that for the executive or judiciary branch of the government.

Were the establishment to be tried by its fruits, are not the daily devotions conducted by these legal ecclesiastics, already degenerating into a scanty attendance, and a tiresome formality!

Rather than let this step beyond the landmarks of power have the effect of a legitimate precedent, it will be better to apply to it the legal aphorism "de minimis non curat lex" [Law does not concern itself with trifles], or to class it cum "maculis quas aut incuria fudit, aut humana parum cavit natura." [with "the stains which either negligence has poured out or which human nature could hardly anticipate."]

Better also to disarm in the same way the precedent of chaplains for the army and navy, than erect them into a political authority in matters of religion. The object of this establishment is seducing; the motive to it is laudable. But is it not safer to adhere to a right principle, and trust to its consequences, than confide in the reasoning however specious in favor of a wrong one. Look through the armies and navies of the world, and say whether in the appointment of their ministers of religion, the spiritual interest of the flocks or the temporal interest of the shepherds, be most in view, whether here, as elsewhere the political care of religion is not a nominal more than a real aid. If the spirit of armies be devout, the spirit out of the armies will never be less so; and a failure of religious instruction and exhortation from a voluntary source within or without will rarely happen; if such be not the spirit of armies, the official services of their teachers are not likely to produce it. It is more likely to flow from the labors of a spontaneous zeal. The armies of the Puritans had their appointed chaplains; but without these there would have been no lack of public devotion in that devout age.

The case of navies with insulated crews may be less within the scope of these reflections. But it is not entirely so. The chance of a devout officer might be of as much worth to religion, as the service of an ordinary chaplain [were it admitted that religion has a real interest in the latter]. But we are always to keep in mind that it is safer to trust the consequences of a right principle than reasoning in support of a bad one.

Religious proclamations by the executive recommending thanksgivings and fasts are shoots from the same root with the legislative acts reviewed.

Although recommendations only, they imply a religious agency, making no part of the trust delegated to political rulers.

The objections to them are,

1. That governments ought not to interpose in relation to those subject to their authority but in cases where they can do it with effect. An advisory government is a contradiction in terms.

2. The members of a government as such can in no sense be regarded as possessing an advisory trust from their constituents in their religious capacities. They cannot form an ecclesiastical assembly, convocation, council, or synod, and as such issue decrees or injunctions addressed to the faith or the consciences of the people. In their individual capacities, as distinct from their official station, they might unite in recommendations of any sort whatever, in the same manner as any other individuals might do. But then their recommendations ought to express the true character from which they emanate.

3. They seem to imply and certainly nourish the erroneous idea of a national religion. The idea just as it related to the Jewish nation under a theocracy, having been improperly adopted by so many nations which have embraced Christianity, is too apt to lurk in the bosoms even of Americans, who in general are aware of the

179

distinction between religious and political societies. The idea also of a union of all to form one nation under one government in acts of devotion to the God of all is an imposing idea. But reason and the principles of the Christian religion require that all the individuals composing a nation even of the same precise creed and wished to unite in a universal act of religion at the same time, the union ought to be effected through the intervention of their religious not of their political representatives. In a nation composed of various sects, some alienated widely from others, and where no agreement could take place through the former, the interposition of the latter is doubly wrong.

4. The tendency of the practice, to narrow the recommendation to the standard of the predominant sect. The first proclamation of General Washington, dated January 1, 1795, recommending a day of thanksgiving, embraced all who believed in a supreme ruler of the universe. That of Mr. Adams called for a Christian worship. Many private letters reproached the proclamations issued by James Madison for using general terms, used in that of President Washington; and some of them for not inserting particulars according with the faith of certain Christian sects. The practice if not strictly guarded naturally terminates in conformity to the creed of the majority and a single sect, if amounting to a majority.

5. The last and not the least objection is the liability of the practice to subservience to political views; to the scandal of religion, as well as the increase of party animosities. Candid or incautious politicians will not always disown such views. In truth it is difficult to frame such a religious proclamation generally suggested by a political state of things, without referring to them in terms having some bearing on party questions. The proclamation of

President Washington which was issued just after the suppression of the insurrection in Pennsylvania and at a time when the public mind was divided on several topics, was so construed by many. Of this the Secretary of State himself, E. Randolph seems to have had anticipation.

The original draft of that instrument [is] filed in the Department of State in the hand writing of Mr. Hamilton, the Secretary of the Treasury. It appears that several slight alterations only had been made at the suggestion of the Secretary of State; and in a marginal note in his hand it is remarked that "In short this proclamation ought to savor as much as possible of religion, and not too much of having a political object." In a subjoined note in the hand of Mr. Hamilton, this remark is answered by the counter-remark that "A proclamation of a government which is a national act, naturally embraces objects which are political" so naturally is the idea of policy associated with religion, whatever be the mode or the occasion, when a function of the latter is assumed by those in power.

During the administration of Mr. Jefferson no religious proclamation was issued. It being understood that his successor was disinclined to such interpositions of the executive and by some supposed moreover that they might originate with more propriety with the legislative body, a resolution was passed requesting him to issue a proclamation.

It was thought not proper to refuse a compliance altogether; but a form and language were employed, which were meant to deaden as much as possible any claim of political right to enjoin religious observances by resting these expressly on the voluntary compliance of individuals, and even by limiting the recommendation to such as wished simultaneous as well as voluntary performance of a religious act on the occasion.

THOMAS JEFFERSON'S FIVE BILLS
ON RELIGION IN THE VIRGINIA STATUTES

Among the best known of Thomas Jefferson's writings is *The Virginia Act for Establishing Religious Freedom*. Written in 1779, the act was written as part of the body of law for the new state of Virginia. Less well-known is that this act was but one bill among five that Jefferson wrote pertaining to religion. The other four bills related to the enforcement of religion by law and provide needed context for an understanding of Jefferson's views.

82. A Bill for Establishing Religious Freedom

Well aware that the opinions and belief of men depend not on their own will, but follow involuntarily the evidence proposed to their minds; that Almighty God has created the mind free, and manifested his supreme will that free it shall remain by making it altogether insusceptible of restraint; that all attempts to influence it by temporal punishments, or burdens, or by civil incapacitations, tend only to beget habits of hypocrisy and meanness, and are a departure from the plan of the holy author of our religion, who being lord both of body and mind, yet chose not to propagate it by coercions on either, as was in his Almighty power to do, but to extend it by its influence on reason alone; that the impious presumption of legislators and rulers, civil as well as ecclesiastical, who, being themselves but fallible and uninspired men, have assumed dominion over the faith of others, setting up their own opinions and modes of thinking as the only true and infallible, and as such endeavoring to impose them on others, has established and maintained false religions over the greatest part of the world and through all time: That to compel a man to furnish contributions of money for the propagation of opinions which he disbelieves and abhors, is sinful and tyrannical; that even the forcing him to support this or that teacher of his own religious persuasion, is depriving him of the comfortable liberty of giving his contributions to the particular pastor whose morals he would make his pattern, and whose powers he feels most persuasive to righteousness; and is withdrawing from the ministry those temporary rewards, which proceeding from an approbation of their personal conduct, are an additional incitement to earnest and unremitting labors for the instruction of mankind; that our civil rights have no dependence on our religious opinions, any more than our opinions in physics or geometry; that therefore the proscribing any citizen as unworthy the public confidence by laying upon him an incapacity of being called to offices of trust and emolument, unless he profess or renounce this or that religious opinion, is depriving him injuriously of those privileges and advantages to which, in common with his fellow citizens, he has a natural right; that it tends also to corrupt the principles of that very religion it is meant to encourage, by bribing, with a monopoly of worldly honors and emoluments, those who will externally profess and conform to it; that though indeed these are criminal who do not withstand such temptation, yet neither are those innocent who lay the bait in their way; that the opinions of men are not the object of civil government, nor under its jurisdiction; that to suffer the civil magistrate to intrude his powers into the field of opinion and to restrain the profession or propagation of principles on supposition of their ill tendency is a dangerous fallacy, which at once destroys all religious liberty, because he being of course judge of that tendency will make his opinions the rule of judgment, and approve or condemn the sentiments of others only as they shall square with or differ from his own; that it is time enough for the rightful purposes of civil government for its officers to interfere when principles break out into overt acts against peace and good order; and finally, that truth is great and will prevail if left to herself; that she is the proper and sufficient antagonist to error, and has nothing to fear from the conflict unless by human interposition disarmed of her natural weapons, free argument and debate; errors ceasing to be dangerous when it is permitted freely to contradict them.

We the General Assembly of Virginia do enact that no man shall be compelled to frequent or support any religious worship, place, or ministry whatsoever, nor shall be enforced, restrained, molested, or burdened in his body or goods, nor shall otherwise suffer, on account of his religious opinions or belief; but that all men shall be free to profess, and by argument to maintain, their opinions in matters of religion, and that the same shall in no wise diminish, enlarge, or affect their civil rights.

And though we well know that this Assembly, elected by the people for the ordinary purposes of legislation only, have no power to restrain the acts of succeeding Assemblies, constituted with powers equal to our own, and that therefore to declare this act irrevocable would be of no effect in law; yet we are free to declare, and do declare, that the rights hereby asserted are of the natural rights of mankind, and that if any act shall be hereafter passed to repeal the present or to narrow its operation, such act will be an infringement of natural right.

83. A Bill for Saving the Property of the Church Heretofore by Law Established

Be it enacted by the General Assembly, that the several tracts of Glebe land, the churches, and chapels, the books, vestments, plate and ornaments, all arrears of money and tobacco, and all property real and personal of private donation, which on the seventh day of October, in the year one thousand seven hundred and seventy six, were vested in any persons whatever for the use of the English church till then established by law, or were due or contracted for, bona fide, on that day, or which since that time have legally become so vested, due, or contracted for, shall be saved in all time to come to the members of the said English church, by whatever denomination they shall henceforth call themselves, who shall be resident within the several parishes as they stood distinguished by metes and bounds on the same day, those of each parish to have the separate and legal property of the said articles belonging to their respective parishes, and to apply them from year to year, by themselves, or by agents to be appointed by themselves as they shall hereafter agree, for and towards the support of their ministry; and that no future change in the form of their church government, ordination of their ministry, or rituals of worship, shall take away or affect the benefit of this saving.

The surviving vestrymen in every parish shall have authority to carry into execution all contracts legally and bona fide made by themselves, or their predecessors, before the first day of January, in the year 1777, and to provide for the payment of all arrears of salaries due to ministers or readers for services performed before that day, by a levy, if they have not already on hand money or tobacco sufficient, and for these purposes may sue or be sued as might have been heretofore where vestries were full.

Where any parish has been altered in its bounds, the inhabitants thereof shall nevertheless remain liable for their proportionate part of all monies or tobacco due, and all contracts legally made, before such division or alteration, to be apportioned on them and levied by the vestry of the respective parish into which they are incorporated by such division or alteration.

And whereas vestries although authorized by law to levy on their parishioners so much only as was sufficient to answer the legal demands on their parish, actually existing, yet frequently levied more, so that there remained on their hands a deposit to be applied to the future uses of their respective parishes, and it may have happened that in some instances such deposits were on hand on the said first day of

January, in the year one thousand seven hundred and seventy seven, after all legal demands satisfied, which were then existing, or which by this act are made legal; and also debts may have been owing to some parishes, Be it therefore enacted, that such deposits and debts shall be applied to the maintenance of the poor of such parishes, where it has not already been done, in case of the poor rates to be levied for that purpose in future; and in the case of any such parish since then divided or altered, or lying in different counties, such easement shall be divided and apportioned in the same way as burdens in a like case are herein before directed to be apportioned. But where any parish has no glebe such deposits and debts, or the proportion thereof, belonging to such parish, shall be applied towards purchasing a glebe, the property and application of which shall be in the same persons and for the same uses, and according to the same rules as would have been by the former part of this act, had the said glebe been purchased before the passing hereof.

84. A Bill for Punishing Disturbers of Religious Worship and Sabbath Breakers

Be it enacted by the General Assembly, that no officer, for any civil cause, shall arrest any minister of the gospel, licensed according to the rules of his sect, and who shall have taken the oath of fidelity to the commonwealth, while such minister shall be publicly preaching or performing religious worship in any church, chapel, or meeting-house, on pain of imprisonment and amercement [punishment], at the discretion of a jury, and of making satisfaction to the party so arrested.

And if any person shall of purpose, maliciously, or contemptuously, disquiet or disturb any congregation assembled in any church, chapel, or meeting-house, or misuse any such minister being there, he may be put under restraint during religious worship by any Justice present, which Justice, if present, or if none be present, then any

Justice before whom proof of the offense shall be made, may cause the offender to find two sureties to be bound by recognizance in a sufficient penalty for his good behavior, and in default thereof shall commit him to prison, there to remain till the next court to be held for the same county; and upon conviction of the said offense before the said court, he shall be further punished by imprisonment and amercement [punishment] at the discretion of a jury.

If any person on Sunday shall himself be found laboring at his own or any other trade or calling, or shall employ his apprentices, servants or slaves in labor, or other business, except it be in the ordinary household offices of daily necessity, or other work of necessity or charity, he shall forfeit the sum of ten shillings for every such offense, deeming every apprentice, servant, or slave so employed, and every day he shall be so employed as constituting a distinct offense.

85. A Bill for Appointing Days of Public Fasting and Thanksgiving

Be it enacted by the General Assembly, that the power of appointing days of public fasting and humiliation, or thanksgiving, throughout this commonwealth, may in the recess of the General Assembly, be exercised by the Governor, or Chief Magistrate, with the advice of the Council; and such appointment shall be notified to the public, by a proclamation, in which the occasion of the fasting or thanksgiving shall be particularly set forth. Every minister of the gospel shall on each day so to be appointed, attend and perform divine service and preach a sermon or discourse suited to the occasion, in his church, on pain of forfeiting fifty pounds for every failure, not having a reasonable excuse.

86. A Bill Annulling Marriages Prohibited by the Levitical Law and Appointing the Mode of Solemnizing Lawful Marriage

Be it enacted by the General Assembly, that marriages prohibited by the Levitical law shall be null; and persons marrying contrary to that prohibition, and cohabiting as man and wife, convicted thereof in the General Court, shall be amerced, from time to time, until they separate. A marriage between a person of free condition and a slave, or between a white person and a negro, or between a white person and a mulatto, shall be null. Where a person, by inquisition taken by virtue of a commission issuing out of the High Court of Chancery, shall be found a lunatic, if, before such person shall be declared of sane mind by the Judges of the said court, or two of them, he or she shall marry, such marriage shall be null. And a marriage between any persons whatsoever, unless it be with such license, and, moreover if both or either of the parties not having been married before, be under the age of twenty one years, with such consent, as herein after directed, shall be null.

The marriage license shall be issued by the clerk of the court of that county, in which the woman shall have resided for the last proceeding four weeks, at the least, in this form or to this effect.

A B, of the hundred of _____ in the county of _____ and C D, of the hundred of _____ in the county of _____ are hereby _____ licensed to be joined together in matrimony;

and shall be signed by the first acting Justice of the Peace, of the same county, who shall then be therein; but the clerk shall not issue the license, until the father or guardian of any party who, not having been lawfully married before, shall be under the age of twenty one years, shall have personally declared, or by writing under his hand and seal, attested by two witnesses, shall have signified his consent to the marriage to the clerk, which consent the clerk shall certify at the foot or on the back of the license, and shall certify in a separate paper to the Justice of the Peace.

Any clerk, required to issue a license without such declaration or signification of the father's or guardian's consent, and doubting whether a

party be of full age, or not, may suspend issuing the license until the then next court day of his county, unless he shall be sooner satisfied, when the fact shall be enquired of by a jury, and according to their verdict he shall govern himself in issuing or refusing the license. Any clerk who shall issue a marriage license, when the parties, or either of them, shall be under the age of twenty one years, without such consent, declared or signified aforesaid, shall be liable to the action of the father or guardian of the infant, or of each infant mentioned in the license, for damages; which damages, in case of a suit brought by the guardian, shall be to the use of the ward; and the clerk shall moreover be deprived of his office.

Persons who having obtained such a license, as before is directed, shall, in presence of witnesses, declare or yield their consent to be married together, shall, without further ceremony, be deemed man and wife, as effectually as if the contract had been solemnized, and the espousals celebrated, in the manner prescribed by the ritual of any church, or according to the custom of any religious society, whereof they are members. The clerk issuing licenses shall keep a correct register of them, and the Justices signing them shall report such signature, within six months thereafter, to the court of his county, which report shall be entered by the clerk in such register; and whosoever shall neglect his duty in these particulars, or any of them, shall be amerced.

JUSTICE WILLIAM REHNQUIST'S DISSENT
IN WALLACE V. JAFFREE

Chief Justice William Rehnquist's dissent from the majority in *Wallace v. Jaffree* is often called the "Anti-*Everson*." Written nearly forty years after *Everson*, the dissent includes an overview of the original intentions of the founding fathers, a critical analysis of the Court's Establishment Clause rulings, and a call for the abandonment of Jefferson's "wall of separation of church and state" metaphor.

Thirty-eight years ago this Court, in *Everson v. Board of Education* summarized its exegesis of Establishment Clause doctrine thus:

"In the words of Jefferson, the clause against establishment of religion by law was intended to erect 'a wall of separation between church and State.'"

This language from *Reynolds*, a case involving the Free Exercise Clause of the First Amendment rather than the Establishment Clause, quoted from Thomas Jefferson's letter to the Danbury Baptist Association the phrase "I contemplate with sovereign reverence that act of the whole American people which declared that their legislature should 'make no law respecting an establishment of religion, or prohibiting the free exercise thereof,' thus building a wall of separation between church and State."

It is impossible to build sound constitutional doctrine upon a mistaken understanding of constitutional history, but unfortunately the Establishment Clause has been expressly freighted with Jefferson's misleading metaphor for nearly 40 years. Thomas Jefferson was of course in France at the time the constitutional Amendments known as

the Bill of Rights were passed by Congress and ratified by the States. His letter to the Danbury Baptist Association was a short note of courtesy, written 14 years after the Amendments were passed by Congress. He would seem to any detached observer as a less than ideal source of contemporary history as to the meaning of the Religion Clauses of the First Amendment.

Jefferson's fellow Virginian, James Madison, with whom he was joined in the battle for the enactment of the Virginia Statute of Religious Liberty of 1786, did play as large a part as anyone in the drafting of the Bill of Rights. He had two advantages over Jefferson in this regard: he was present in the United States, and he was a leading Member of the First Congress. But when we turn to the record of the proceedings in the First Congress leading up to the adoption of the Establishment Clause of the Constitution, including Madison's significant contributions thereto, we see a far different picture of its purpose than the highly simplified "wall of separation between church and State."

During the debates in the Thirteen Colonies over ratification of the Constitution, one of the arguments frequently used by opponents of ratification was that without a Bill of Rights guaranteeing individual liberty the new general Government carried with it a potential for tyranny. The typical response to this argument on the part of those who favored ratification was that the general Government established by the Constitution had only delegated powers, and that these delegated powers were so limited that the Government would have no occasion to violate individual liberties. This response satisfied some, but not others, and of the 11 Colonies which ratified the Constitution by early 1789, 5 proposed one or another amendments guaranteeing individual liberty. Three—New Hampshire, New York, and Virginia—included in one form or another a declaration of religious freedom. Rhode Island and North Carolina flatly refused to ratify the Constitution in the absence of amendments in the nature of a Bill of Rights. Virginia and North Carolina proposed identical guarantees of religious freedom:

> "All men have an equal, natural and unalienable right to the free exercise of religion, according to the dictates of conscience, and no particular religious sect or society ought to be favored or established, by law, in preference to others."

On June 8, 1789, James Madison rose in the House of Representatives and "reminded the House that this was the day that he had heretofore named for bringing forward amendments to the Constitution." Madison's subsequent remarks in urging the House to adopt his drafts of the proposed amendments were less those of a dedicated advocate of the wisdom of such measures than those of a prudent statesman seeking the enactment of measures sought by a number of his fellow citizens which could surely do no harm and might do a great deal of good. He said:

> "It appears to me that this House is bound by every motive of prudence, not to let the first session pass over without proposing to the State Legislatures, some things to be incorporated into the Constitution, that will render it as acceptable to the whole people of the United States, as it has been found acceptable to a majority of them. I wish, among other reasons why something should be done, that those who had been friendly to the adoption of this Constitution may have the opportunity of proving to those who were opposed to it that they were as sincerely devoted to liberty and a Republican Government, as those who charged them with wishing the adoption of this Constitution in order to lay the foundation of an aristocracy or despotism. It will be a desirable

thing to extinguish from the bosom of every member of the community, any apprehensions that there are those among his countrymen who wish to deprive them of the liberty for which they valiantly fought and honorably bled. And if there are amendments desired of such a nature as will not injure the Constitution, and they can be engrafted so as to give satisfaction to the doubting part of our fellow citizens, the friends of the Federal Government will evince that spirit of deference and concession for which they have hitherto been distinguished."

The language Madison proposed for what ultimately became the Religion Clauses of the First Amendment was this:

"The civil rights of none shall be abridged on account of religious belief or worship, nor shall any national religion be established, nor shall the full and equal rights of conscience be in any manner, or on any pretext, infringed."

On the same day that Madison proposed them, the amendments which formed the basis for the Bill of Rights were referred by the House to a Committee of the Whole, and after several weeks' delay were then referred to a Select Committee consisting of Madison and 10 others. The Committee revised Madison's proposal regarding the establishment of religion to read:

"No religion shall be established by law, nor shall the equal rights of conscience be infringed."

The Committee's proposed revisions were debated in the House on August 15, 1789. The entire debate on the Religion Clauses is contained in two full columns of the "Annals," and does not seem particularly illuminating. Representative Peter Sylvester of New York expressed his dislike for the revised version, because it might have a tendency "to abolish religion altogether." Representative John Vining suggested that the two parts of the sentence be transposed; Representative Elbridge Gerry thought the language should be changed to read "that no religious doctrine shall be established by law." Roger Sherman of Connecticut had the traditional reason for opposing provisions of a Bill of Rights—that Congress had no delegated authority to "make religious establishments"—and therefore he opposed the adoption of the amendment. Representative Daniel Carroll of Maryland thought it desirable to adopt the words proposed, saying "he would not contend with gentlemen about the phraseology, his object was to secure the substance in such a manner as to satisfy the wishes of the honest part of the community."

Madison then spoke, and said that "he apprehended the meaning of the words to be, that Congress should not establish a religion, and enforce the legal observation of it by law, nor compel men to worship God in any manner contrary to their conscience." He said that some of the state conventions had thought that Congress might rely on the Necessary and Proper Clause to infringe the rights of conscience or to establish a national religion, and "to prevent these effects he presumed the amendment was intended, and he thought it as well expressed as the nature of the language would admit."

Representative Benjamin Huntington then expressed the view that the Committee's language might "be taken in such latitude as to be extremely hurtful to the cause of religion. He understood the amendment to mean what had been expressed by the gentleman from Virginia; but others might find it convenient to put another construction upon it." Huntington, from Connecticut, was concerned that in the New England States, where state-established religions were the rule rather than the exception, the federal courts might not be able to entertain claims based upon an obligation under the bylaws of a religious organization to contribute to the support of a minister or the building of a place of worship. He hoped that "the amendment would be made in such a way as to secure the rights of conscience, and a free exercise of the rights of religion, but not to patronize those who professed no religion at all."

Madison responded that the insertion of the word "national" before the word "religion" in the Committee version should satisfy the minds of those who had criticized the language. "He believed that the people feared one sect might obtain a pre-eminence, or two combine together, and establish a religion to which they would compel others to conform. He thought that if the word 'national' was introduced, it would point the amendment directly to the object it was intended to prevent." Representative Samuel Livermore expressed himself as dissatisfied with Madison's proposed amendment, and thought it would be better if the Committee language were altered to read that "Congress shall make no laws touching religion, or infringing the rights of conscience."

Representative Gerry spoke in opposition to the use of the word "national" because of strong feelings expressed during the ratification debates that a federal government, not a national government, was created by the Constitution. Madison thereby withdrew his proposal but insisted that his reference to a "national religion" only referred to a national establishment and did not mean that the Government was a national one. The question was taken on Representative Livermore's motion, which passed by a vote of 31 for and 20 against.

The following week, without any apparent debate, the House voted to alter the language of the Religion Clauses to read "Congress shall make no law establishing religion, or to prevent the free exercise thereof, or to infringe the rights of conscience." The floor debates in the Senate were secret, and therefore not reported in the Annals. The Senate on September 3, 1789, considered several different forms of the Religion Amendment, and reported this language back to the House:

"Congress shall make no law establishing articles of faith or a mode of worship, or prohibiting the free exercise of religion."

The House refused to accept the Senate's changes in the Bill of Rights and asked for a conference; the version which emerged from the conference was that which ultimately found its way into the Constitution as a part of the First Amendment.

"Congress shall make no law respecting an establishment of religion, or prohibiting the free exercise thereof."

The House and the Senate both accepted this language on successive days, and the Amendment was proposed in this form.

On the basis of the record of these proceedings in the House of Representatives, James Madison was undoubtedly the most important architect among the Members of the House of the Amendments which became the Bill of Rights, but it was James Madison speaking as an advocate of sensible legislative compromise, not as an advocate of incorporating the Virginia Statute of Religious Liberty into the United States Constitution. During the ratification debate in the Virginia Convention, Madison had actually opposed the idea of any Bill of Rights. His sponsorship of the Amendments in the House was obviously not that of a zealous believer in the necessity of the Religion Clauses, but of one who felt it might do some good, could do no harm, and would satisfy those who had ratified the Constitution on the condition that Congress propose a Bill of Rights. His original language "nor shall any national religion be established" obviously does not conform to the "wall of separation" between church and State idea which latter-day commentators have ascribed to him. His explanation on the floor of the meaning of his language—"that Congress should not establish a religion, and enforce the legal observation of it by law" is of the same ilk. When he replied to Huntington in the debate over the proposal which came from the Select Committee of the House, he urged that the language "no religion shall be established by law" should be amended by inserting the word "national" in front of the word "religion."

It seems indisputable from these glimpses of Madison's thinking, as reflected by actions on the floor of the House in 1789, that he saw the Amendment as designed to prohibit the establishment of a national religion, and perhaps to prevent discrimination among sects. He did not see it as requiring neutrality on the part of government between religion and irreligion. Thus the Court's opinion in *Everson*—while correct in bracketing Madison and Jefferson together in their exertions in their home State leading to the enactment of the Virginia Statute of Religious Liberty—is totally incorrect in suggesting that Madison carried these views onto the floor of the United States House of Representatives when he proposed the language which would ultimately become the Bill of Rights.

The repetition of this error in the Court's opinion in *Illinois ex rel. McCollum v. Board of Education* does not make it any sounder historically. Finally, in *Abington School District v. Schempp*, the Court made the truly remarkable statement that "the views of Madison and Jefferson, preceded by Roger Williams, came to be incorporated not only in the Federal Constitution but likewise in those of most of our States". On the basis of what evidence we have, this statement is demonstrably incorrect as a matter of history. And its repetition in varying forms in succeeding opinions of the Court can give it no more authority than it possesses as a matter of fact; *stare decisis* [to stand by decided matters] may bind courts as to matters of law, but it cannot bind them as to matters of history.

None of the other Members of Congress who spoke during the August 15th debate expressed the slightest indication that they thought the language before them from the Select Committee, or the evil to be aimed at, would require that the Government be absolutely neutral as between religion and irreligion. The evil to be aimed at, so far as those who spoke are concerned, appears to have been the establishment of a national church, and perhaps the preference of one religious sect over another; but it was definitely not concerned about whether the Government might aid all religions evenhandedly. If one were to follow the advice of Justice Brennan, concurring in *Abington School District v. Schemp*, and construe the Amendment in the light of what particular "practices . . . challenged threaten those consequences which the Framers deeply feared; whether, in short, they tend to promote that type of interdependence between religion and state which the First Amendment was designed to prevent," one would have to say that the First Amendment Establishment Clause should be read no more broadly than to prevent the establishment of a national religion or the governmental preference of one religious sect over another.

The actions of the First Congress, which reenacted the Northwest Ordinance for the governance of the Northwest Territory in 1789, confirm the view that Congress did not mean that the Government should be neutral between religion and irreligion. The House of Representatives took up the Northwest Ordinance on the same day as Madison introduced his proposed amendments which became the Bill of Rights; while at that time the Federal Government was of course not bound by draft amendments to the Constitution which had not yet been proposed by Congress, say nothing of ratified by the States, it seems highly unlikely that the House of Representatives would simultaneously consider proposed amendments to the Constitution and enact an important piece of territorial legislation which conflicted with the intent of those proposals. The Northwest Ordinance reenacted the Northwest Ordinance of 1787 and provided that "religion, morality, and knowledge, being necessary to good government and the happiness of mankind, schools and the means of education shall forever be encouraged." Land grants for schools in the Northwest Territory were not limited to public schools. It was not until 1845 that Congress limited land grants in the new States and Territories to nonsectarian schools.

On the day after the House of Representatives voted to adopt the form of the First Amendment Religion Clauses which was ultimately proposed and ratified, Representative Elias Boudinot proposed a resolution asking President George Washington to issue a Thanksgiving Day Proclamation. Boudinot said he "could not think of letting the session pass over without offering an opportunity to all the citizens of the United States of joining with one voice, in returning to Almighty God their sincere thanks for the many blessings he had poured down upon them." Representative Aedanas Burke objected to the resolution because he did not like "this mimicking of European customs"; Representative Thomas Tucker objected that whether or not the people had reason to be satisfied with the Constitution was something that the States knew better than the Congress, and in any event "it is a religious matter, and, as such, is proscribed to us." Representative Sherman supported the resolution "not only as a laudable one in itself, but as warranted by a number of precedents in Holy Writ: for instance, the solemn thanksgivings and rejoicings which took place in the time of Solomon, after the building of the temple, was a case in point. This example, he thought, worthy of Christian imitation on the present occasion. . . ."

Boudinot's resolution was carried in the affirmative on September 25, 1789. Boudinot and Sherman, who favored the Thanksgiving Proclamation, voted in favor of the adoption of the proposed amendments to the Constitution, including the Religion Clauses; Tucker, who opposed the Thanksgiving Proclamation, voted against the adoption of the amendments which became the Bill of Rights.

Within two weeks of this action by the House, George Washington responded to the Joint Resolution which by now had been changed to include the language that the President "recommend to the people of the United States a day of public thanksgiving and prayer, to be observed by acknowledging with grateful hearts the many and signal favors of Almighty God, especially by affording them an opportunity peaceably to establish a form of government for their safety and happiness." The Presidential Proclamation was couched in these words:

Now, therefore, I do recommend and assign Thursday, the 26th day of November next, to be devoted by the people of these States to the service of that great and glorious Being who is the beneficent author of all the good that was, that is, or that will be; that we may then all unite in rendering unto Him our sincere and humble thanks for His kind care and protection of the people of this country previous to their becoming a nation; for the signal and manifold mercies and the favorable interpositions of His providence in the course and conclusion of the late war; for the great degree of tranquility, union, and plenty which we have since enjoyed; for the peaceable and rational manner in which we have been enabled to establish constitutions of government for our safety and happiness, and particularly the national one now lately instituted; for the civil and religious liberty with which we are blessed, and the means we have of acquiring and diffusing useful knowledge; and, in general, for all the great and various favors which He has been pleased to confer upon us.

And also that we may then unite in most humbly offering our prayers and supplications to the great Lord and Ruler of Nations, and beseech Him to pardon our national and other transgressions; to enable us all, whether in public or private stations, to perform our several and relative duties properly and punctually; to render our National Government a blessing to all the people by constantly being a Government of wise, just, and constitutional laws, discreetly and faithfully executed and obeyed; to protect and guide all sovereigns and nations (especially such as have shown kindness to us), and to bless them with good governments, peace, and concord; to promote the knowledge and practice of true religion and virtue, and the increase of science among them and us; and, generally, to grant unto all mankind such a degree of temporal prosperity as He alone knows to be best.

George Washington, John Adams, and James Madison all issued Thanksgiving Proclamations; Thomas Jefferson did not, saying:

Fasting and prayer are religious exercises; the enjoining them an act of discipline. Every religious society has a right to determine for itself the times for these exercises, and the objects proper for them, according to their own particular tenets; and this right can never be safer than in their own hands, where the Constitution has deposited it.

As the United States moved from the 18th into the 19th century, Congress appropriated time and again public moneys in support of sectarian Indian education carried on by religious organizations. Typical of these was Jefferson's treaty with the Kaskaskia Indians, which provided annual cash support for the Tribe's Roman Catholic priest and church. It was not until 1897, when aid to sectarian education for Indians had reached $500,000 annually, that Congress decided thereafter to cease appropriating money for education in sectarian schools. This history shows the fallacy of the notion found in *Everson* that "no tax in any amount" may be levied for religious activities in any form.

Joseph Story, a Member of this Court from 1811 to 1845, and during much of that time a professor at the Harvard Law School, published by far the most comprehensive treatise on the United States Constitution that had then appeared. Volume 2 of Story's Commentaries on the

Constitution of the United States discussed the meaning of the Establishment Clause of the First Amendment this way

> Probably at the time of the adoption of the Constitution, and of the amendment to it now under consideration [First Amendment], the general if not the universal sentiment in America was, that Christianity ought to receive encouragement from the State so far as was not incompatible with the private rights of conscience and the freedom of religious worship. An attempt to level all religions, and to make it a matter of state policy to hold all in utter indifference, would have created universal disapprobation, if not universal indignation.

* * *

> The real object of the First Amendment was not to countenance, much less to advance, Mahometanism, or Judaism, or infidelity, by prostrating Christianity; but to exclude all rivalry among Christian sects, and to prevent any national ecclesiastical establishment which should give to a hierarchy the exclusive patronage of the national government. It thus cut off the means of religious persecution (the vice and pest of former ages), and of the subversion of the rights of conscience in matters of religion, which had been trampled upon almost from the days of the Apostles to the present age. . . .

Thomas Cooley's eminence as a legal authority rivaled that of Story. Cooley stated in his treatise entitled Constitutional Limitations that aid to a particular religious sect was prohibited by the United States Constitution, but he went on to say:

> But while thus careful to establish, protect, and defend religious freedom and equality, the American constitutions contain no

provisions which prohibit the authorities from such solemn recognition of a superintending Providence in public transactions and exercises as the general religious sentiment of mankind inspires, and as seems meet and proper in finite and dependent beings. Whatever may be the shades of religious belief, all must acknowledge the fitness of recognizing in important human affairs the superintending care and control of the Great Governor of the Universe, and of acknowledging with thanksgiving his boundless favors, or bowing in contrition when visited with the penalties of his broken laws. No principle of constitutional law is violated when thanksgiving or fast days are appointed; when chaplains are designated for the army and navy; when legislative sessions are opened with prayer or the reading of the Scriptures, or when religious teaching is encouraged by a general exemption of the houses of religious worship from taxation for the support of State government. Undoubtedly the spirit of the Constitution will require, in all these cases, that care be taken to avoid discrimination in favor of or against any one religious denomination or sect; but the power to do any of these things does not become unconstitutional simply because of its susceptibility to abuse. . . .

Cooley added that

this public recognition of religious worship, however, is not based entirely, perhaps not even mainly, upon a sense of what is due to the Supreme Being himself as the author of all good and of all law; but the same reasons of state policy which induce the government to aid institutions of charity and seminaries of instruction will incline it also to foster religious worship and religious institutions, as conservators of the public morals and valuable, if not indispensable, assistants to the preservation of the public order.

It would seem from this evidence that the Establishment Clause of the First Amendment had acquired a well-accepted meaning: it forbade establishment of a national religion, and forbade preference among religious sects or denominations. Indeed, the first American dictionary defined the word "establishment" as "the act of establishing, founding, ratifying or ordaining," such as in "the episcopal form of religion, so called, in England." The Establishment Clause did not require government neutrality between religion and irreligion nor did it prohibit the Federal Government from providing nondiscriminatory aid to religion. There is simply no historical foundation for the proposition that the Framers intended to build the "wall of separation" that was constitutionalized in *Everson*.

Notwithstanding the absence of a historical basis for this theory of rigid separation, the wall idea might well have served as a useful albeit misguided analytical concept, had it led this Court to unified and principled results in Establishment Clause cases. The opposite, unfortunately, has been true; in the 38 years since *Everson* our Establishment Clause cases have been neither principled nor unified. Our recent opinions, many of them hopelessly divided pluralities, have with embarrassing candor conceded that the "wall of separation" is merely a "blurred, indistinct, and variable barrier," which "is not wholly accurate" and can only be "dimly perceived."

Whether due to its lack of historical support or its practical unworkability, the *Everson* "wall" has proved all but useless as a guide to sound constitutional adjudication. It illustrates only too well the wisdom of Benjamin Cardozo's observation that "metaphors in law are to be narrowly watched, for starting as devices to liberate thought, they end often by enslaving it."

But the greatest injury of the "wall" notion is its mischievous diversion of judges from the actual intentions of the drafters of the Bill of Rights. The "crucible of litigation" is well adapted to adjudicating factual disputes on the basis of testimony presented in court, but no amount of repetition of historical errors in judicial opinions can make the errors true. The "wall of separation between church and State" is a metaphor based on bad history, a metaphor which has proved useless as a guide to judging. It should be frankly and explicitly abandoned.

The Court has more recently attempted to add some mortar to *Everson*'s wall through the three-part test of *Lemon v. Kurtzman*, which served at first to offer a more useful test for purposes of the Establishment Clause than did the "wall" metaphor. Generally stated, the *Lemon* test proscribes state action that has a sectarian purpose or effect, or causes an impermissible governmental entanglement with religion.

Lemon cited *Board of Education v. Allen*, as the source of the "purpose" and "effect" prongs of the three-part test. The *Allen* opinion explains, however, how it inherited the purpose and effect elements from *Schempp* and *Everson*, both of which contain the historical errors described above. Thus the purpose and effect prongs have the same historical deficiencies as the wall concept itself: they are in no way based on either the language or intent of the drafters.

The secular purpose prong has proven mercurial in application because it has never been fully defined, and we have never fully stated how the test is to operate. If the purpose prong is intended to void those aids to sectarian institutions accompanied by a stated legislative purpose to aid religion, the prong will condemn nothing so long as the legislature utters a secular purpose and says nothing about aiding religion. Thus the constitutionality of a statute may depend upon what the legislators put into the legislative history and, more importantly, what they leave out. The purpose prong means little if it only requires the legislature to express any secular purpose and omit all sectarian references, because legislators might do just that. Faced with a valid legislative secular purpose, we could not properly ignore that purpose without a factual basis for doing so.

However, if the purpose prong is aimed to void all statutes enacted with the intent to aid sectarian institutions, whether stated or not, then most statutes providing any aid, such as textbooks or bus rides for sectarian school children, will fail because one of the purposes behind every statute, whether stated or not, is to aid the target of its largesse. In other words, if the purpose prong requires an absence of *any* intent to aid sectarian institutions, whether or not expressed, few state laws in this area could pass the test, and we would be required to void some state aids to religion which we have already upheld.

The entanglement prong of the *Lemon* test came from *Walz v. Tax Comm'n. Walz* involved a constitutional challenge to New York's time-honored practice of providing state property tax exemptions to church property used in worship. The *Walz* opinion refused to "undermine the ultimate constitutional objective of the Establishment Clause as illuminated by history," and upheld the tax exemption. The Court examined the historical relationship between the State and church when church property was in issue, and determined that the challenged tax exemption did not so entangle New York with the church as to cause an intrusion or interference with religion. Interferences with religion should arguably be dealt with under the Free Exercise Clause, but the entanglement inquiry in *Walz* was consistent with that case's broad survey of the relationship between state taxation and religious property.

We have not always followed *Walz's* reflective inquiry into entanglement, however. One of the difficulties with the entanglement prong is that, when divorced from the logic of *Walz*, it creates an "insoluable paradox" in school aid cases: we have required aid to parochial schools to be closely watched lest it be put to sectarian use, yet this close supervision itself will create an entanglement. For example, in *Wolman*, the Court in part struck the State's nondiscriminatory provision of buses for parochial school field trips, because the state supervision of sectarian officials in charge of field trips would be too onerous. This type of self-defeating result is certainly not required to ensure that States do not establish religions.

The entanglement test as applied in cases like *Wolman* also ignores the myriad state administrative regulations properly placed upon sectarian institutions such as curriculum, attendance, and certification requirements for sectarian schools, or fire and safety regulations for churches. Avoiding entanglement between church and State may be an important consideration in a case like *Walz*, but if the entanglement prong were applied to all state and church relations in the automatic manner in which it has been applied to school aid cases, the State could hardly require anything of church-related institutions as a condition for receipt of financial assistance.

These difficulties arise because the *Lemon* test has no more grounding in the history of the First Amendment than does the wall theory upon which it rests. The three-part test represents a determined effort to craft a workable rule from a historically faulty doctrine; but the rule can only be as sound as the doctrine it attempts to service. The three-part test has simply not provided adequate standards for deciding Establishment Clause cases, as this Court has slowly come to realize. Even worse, the *Lemon* test has caused this Court to fracture into unworkable plurality opinions depending upon how each of the three factors applies to a certain state action. The results from our school services cases show the difficulty we have encountered in making the *Lemon* test yield principled results.

For example, a State may lend to parochial school children geography textbooks that contain maps of the United States, but the State may not lend maps of the United States for use in geography class. A State may lend textbooks on American colonial history, but it may not lend a film on George Washington, or a film projector to show it in history class. A State may lend classroom workbooks, but may not lend workbooks in which the parochial school children write, thus rendering them nonreusable. A State may pay for bus transportation to religious schools but may not pay for bus transportation from the parochial school to the public zoo or natural history museum for a field trip. A State may pay for diagnostic services conducted in the parochial school but therapeutic services must be given in a different building; speech and hearing "services" conducted by the State inside the sectarian school are forbidden, but the State may conduct speech and hearing diagnostic testing inside the sectarian school. Exceptional parochial school students may receive counseling, but it must take place outside of the parochial school, such as in a trailer parked down the street. A State may give cash to a parochial school to pay for the administration of state-written tests and state-ordered reporting services, but it may not provide funds for teacher-prepared tests on secular subjects. Religious instruction may not be given in public school, but the public school may release students during the day for religion classes elsewhere, and may enforce attendance at those classes with its truancy laws.

These results violate the historically sound principle "that the Establishment Clause does not forbid governments ... to provide general welfare under which benefits are distributed to private individuals, even though many of those individuals may elect to use those benefits in ways that 'aid' religious instruction or worship." It is not surprising in the light of this record that our most recent opinions have expressed doubt on the usefulness of the *Lemon* test.

Although the test initially provided helpful assistance, we soon began describing the test as only a "guideline," and lately we have described it as "no more than a useful signpost." We have noted that the *Lemon* test is "not easily applied," and under the *Lemon* test we have "sacrificed clarity and predictability for flexibility." In *Lynch* we reiterated that the *Lemon* test has never been binding on the Court, and we cited two cases where we had declined to apply it.

If a constitutional theory has no basis in the history of the amendment it seeks to interpret, is difficult to apply and yields unprincipled results, I see little use in it. The "crucible of litigation" has produced only consistent unpredictability, and today's effort is just a continuation of "the sisyphean task of trying to patch together the 'blurred, indistinct and variable barrier' described in *Lemon v. Kurtzman*." We have done much straining since 1947, but still we admit that we can only "dimly perceive" the *Everson* wall. Our perception has been clouded not by the Constitution but by the mists of an unnecessary metaphor.

The true meaning of the Establishment Clause can only be seen in its history. As drafters of our Bill of Rights, the Framers inscribed the principles that control today. Any deviation from their intentions frustrates the permanence of that Charter and will only lead to the type of unprincipled decision-making that has plagued our Establishment Clause cases since *Everson*.

The Framers intended the Establishment Clause to prohibit the designation of any church as a "national" one. The Clause was also designed to stop the Federal Government from asserting a preference for one religious denomination or sect over others. Given the "incorporation" of the Establishment Clause as against the States via the Fourteenth Amendment in *Everson*, States are prohibited as well from establishing a religion or discriminating between sects. As its history abundantly shows, however, nothing in the Establishment Clause requires government to be strictly neutral between religion and irreligion, nor does that Clause prohibit Congress or the States from pursuing legitimate secular ends through nondiscriminatory sectarian means.

The Court strikes down the Alabama statute because the State wished to "characterize prayer as a favored practice." It would come as much of a shock to those who drafted the Bill of Rights as it will to a large number of thoughtful Americans today to learn that the Constitution, as construed by the majority, prohibits the Alabama Legislature from "endorsing" prayer. George Washington himself, at the request of the very Congress which passed the Bill of Rights, proclaimed a day of "public thanksgiving and prayer, to be observed by acknowl-edging with grateful hearts the many and signal favors of Almighty God." History must judge whether it was the Father of his Country in 1789, or a majority of the Court today, which has strayed from the meaning of the Establishment Clause.

The State surely has a secular interest in regulating the manner in which public schools are conducted. Nothing in the Establishment Clause of the First Amendment, properly understood, prohibits any such generalized "endorsement" of prayer. I would therefore reverse the judgment of the Court of Appeals.

NOTES

Introduction
1. *Everson v. Board of Education*, 330 U.S. 1 (1947).
2. Shakespeare, *King Henry VI*, Part II, Act IV, Scene 2.
3. "Characters from 'The Simpsons' More Well Known to Americans Than Their First Amendment Freedoms, Survey Finds," McCormick Tribune Freedom Museum, 1 March, 2006, http://www.mccormicktribune.org/ news/2006/pr030106.aspx.

Chapter 1
1. This vignette is composed from descriptions in Thomas Carlyle's *The French Revolution*, Richard Hooke's *The Reign of Terror* (Pullman, WA: WSU Press, 1999), and the *Dictionary of Phrase and Fable*, ed. by E. Cobham Brewer (New York: Stattler and Jones, 1898).
2. During the French Revolution, there were a number of women known for playing the role of Goddess of Reason. The actress who portrayed the goddess in the enthronement ceremony in Notre Dame was Mademoiselle Malliard, though the most popular goddess was the wife of a printer named Momoro. Statues of such women as the Goddess of Liberty replaced statues of the Virgin Mary on the altars of France during the Revolution, and these grew so popular that they became the model for the Statue of Liberty, which France gave to the United States in honor of its Centennial celebration on 28 October, 1886.

   So deep was the French disdain for religion during these years that Notre Dame fell into horrible disrepair. This was not reversed when Napoleon restored Christian worship to the Cathedral in 1802. Instead, it was not until Victor Hugo described the ravages of Notre Dame in his masterpiece, *The Hunchback of Notre Dame*, that a campaign was launched to restore and save the cathedral. [From E. Cobham Brewer, ed., *Dictionary of Phrase and Fable* (New York: Stattler and Jones, 1898); see also Carlyle: *French Revolution*, Vol. III. Book 4).]
3. Eminent American historian Gary Wills has said, "There were two great revolutions against European monarchs in the late eighteenth century. In the first, the French nation helped Americans achieve their independence from George III. Without that help, our revolution could not have succeeded. Yet when the French rebelled against Louis XVI, Americans at first merely hailed their actions, then hesitated over it, and finally recoiled from it" (*American Heritage*, August 1989).
4. Quoted in Henry Cabot Lodge, *Alexander Hamilton* (New York: Charles Scribner's Sons, 1899, 1922), 253–54.

5. Quoted in Robert L. Cord, *Separation of Church and State* (New York: Lambeth Press, 1982), ix.

6. Peter B. Levy, ed., *100 Key Documents in American Democracy* (Westport, CT: Greenwood Press, 1994), 6.

7. Ibid., 10–11.

8. Quoted in R. E. McMaster, *Wealth for All* (Whitefish: A.N., Inc., 1982), 85.

9. Levy, *100 Key Documents*, 71.

10. Henry Steele Commager, ed., *Documents of American History* (New York: Appleton-Century-Crofts, Inc., 1949), 131.

11. Gregg Singer, *From Rationalism to Irrationality* (Phillipsburg, NJ: Presbyterian and Reformed Publishing Company, 1979), 77–78.

12. Alexander Hamilton, "The Federalist," No. 84, Sec. 11, quoted in Jacob E. Cooke, ed., *The Federalist* (Middletown, PA: Wesleyan University Press, 1961), 579.

13. Leter from Thomas Jefferson to James Madison, 20 December 1787, in Adrienne Koch and William Peden, *The Life and Selected Writings of Thomas Jefferson* (New York: Random House, 1944), 437–38.

14. Robert Allen Rutland, *The Birth of the Bill of Rights, 1776–1791* (Chapel Hill, NC: The University of North Carolina Press, 1955), 164.

15. Joseph Gales, ed., *The Debates and Proceedings in the Congress of the United States, Compiled from Authentic Materials, I* (Washington DC: Gales and Seaton, 1834), 432. (Hereinafter referred to as *Annals I.*)

16. Carl Van Doren, *The Great Rehearsal* (New York: Viking Press, 1948), 238.

17. *Annals I*, 434.

18. Carl Bridenbaugh, *Mitre and Sceptre: Transatlantic Faiths, Ideas, Personalities and Politics* (London: Oxford University Press, 1962), 244.

19. For more on the life of George Whitefield and his American legacy, see the author's book, *Forgotten Founding Father: The Heroic Legacy of George Whitefield* (Nashville: Cumberland House Press, 2001).

20. *Annals I*, 729.

21. Ibid. 730.

22. Ibid. 766.

23. Ibid. 914.

24. Presidential Proclamation, 3 October 1789, in James D. Richardson, ed., *A Compilation of the Messages and Papers of the Presidents, I* (New York: Bureau of National Literature, 1897), 56.

25. *Annals I*, 915.

26. Joseph Story, *Commentaries on the Constitution of the United States*, 2nd ed., Vol. II (Boston: Charles C. Little and James Brown, 1851), sec. 1874, 593.

27. Ibid., sec. 1877, 594.

Chapter 2

1. This vignette is compiled from accounts in Charles Moore, *The Family Life of George Washington* (Boston: Houghton Mifflin, 1926), 167; C. A. Browne, "Elder John Leland and the Mammoth Cheshire Cheese," *Agricultural History* 18 (1944); L. H. Butterfield, "Elder John Leland, Jeffersonian Itinerant," *Proceedings of the American Antiquarian Society* 62 (1952), 214–16.

2. The letters "O.S." appearing after dates stand for "Old Style." In 1752, the Julian or Old Style calendar was replaced in England and her colonies by the Gregorian or New Style calendar, which is still in use today. This added eleven days to the date to bring the calendar year into step with the astronomical year. Thomas Jefferson's birthday, then, which was April 2 under the Old Style calendar, is now celebrated on April 13.

3. Letter from a committee of the Danbury Baptist association to Thomas Jefferson, 7 October 1801, *The Papers of Thomas Jefferson* (Manuscript Division, Library of Congress), Series 1, Box 87, 30 August 1801–15 October 1801.

4. Letter from Levi Lincoln to Thomas Jefferson, 1 January 1801, *The Papers of Thomas Jefferson* (Manuscript Division, Library of Congress), Series 1, Box 89, 2 December 1802–1 January 1802.

5. Ibid.

6. Letter from Thomas Jefferson to Messrs. Nehemiah Dodge, Ephraim Robbins, and Stephen S. Nelson, a committee of the Danbury Baptist association in the state of Connecticut, 1 January 1802, *The Papers of Thomas Jefferson* (Manuscript Division, Library of Congress), Series 1, Box 89, 2 December 1801–1 January 1802.

7. Letter from Thomas Jefferson to the Reverend Samuel Miller, 23 January, 1808, *The Writings of Thomas Jefferson*, ed. Andrew A. Lipscomb and Albert Ellery Bergh, 20 vols. (Washington DC: Thomas Jefferson Memorial Association, 1905), 11:428. (Hereinafter referred to as *Writings of Jefferson.*)

8. Jefferson, Second Inaugural Address, 4 March 1805, *Writings of Jefferson*, 3:378.

9. Letter from Thomas Jefferson to Mrs. John Adams, 11 September 1804, *Writings of Jefferson*, 11:51.

10. *Barron v. City Council of Baltimore*, 32 U.S. (7 Peters) 243, 250 (1833).

11. *Permoli v. Municipality No. 1 of the City of New Orleans*, 44 U.S. (3 Howard) 589, 609 (1845).

12. Joseph Story, *Commentaries on the Constitution of the United States*, 3 vols. (Boston: Hilliard, Gray, 1833), 3:730, sec. 1873.

13. Story, *Commentaries on the Constitution of the United States*, 3:731, sec. 1873.

14. Lincoln wrote these words in a letter to Horace Greeley: "My paramount object in this struggle is to save the Union, and is not either to save or to destroy slavery. If I could save the Union without freeing any slave I would do it, and if I could save it by freeing all the slaves I would do it; and if I could save it by freeing some and leaving others alone I would also do that. What I do about slavery, and the colored race, I do because I believe it helps to save the Union; and what I forbear, I forbear because I do not believe it would help to save the Union. I shall do less whenever I shall believe what I am doing hurts the cause, and I shall do more whenever I shall believe doing more will help the cause." *The Collected Works of Abraham Lincoln*, ed. by Roy P. Basler, Vol. V, "Letter to Horace Greeley" (22 August 1862), 388.

15. Thomas Jefferson, *Notes on Virginia*, 199.

16. William Waller Hening, *The Statutes at Large; Being a Collection of All the Laws of Virginia*, Vol. IXX (Richmond: Printed for the editor by J. & G. Cochran, 1821), 175–77.

17. Richard Peters, Esq., ed., *The Public Statutes at Large of the United States of America*, Vol. VII (Boston: Charles C. Little and James Brown, 1848), 78–79.

18. *American State Papers*, Class VIII, Public Lands, Vol. III, *Documents Legislative and Executive, of the Congress of the United States*, op. cit., 17th Congress, 2nd Session, Document No. 374, "Application of the United Brethren to Be Divested of the Trust Estate of the Lands Conveyed for the Benefit of Certain Christian Indians," 714.

19. James H. Hutson, *Religion and the Founding of the American Republic* (Washington DC: The Library of Congress, 1998), 83.

20. Edwin S. Gaustad, *Sworn on the Altar of God: A Religious Biography of Thomas Jefferson* (Grand Rapids: Eerdmans, 1996), 124.

21. Ibid., x.

22. Hutson, *Religion*, 91.

23. *Federal Orrery*, Boston, 2 July 1795, 2.

24. John Quincy Adams, *Memoirs of John Quincy Adams*, Charles Francis Adams, ed., Vol. I(Philadelphia: J. B. Lippincott and Company, 1874), 268, 30 October 1803.

25. Galliard Hung, ed., *The First Forty Years of Washington Society* (New York: Charles Scribner's Sons, 1906), 16.

26. Hutson, *Religion*, 93.

27. Hung, *First Forty Years*, 13.

28. Letter from Catharine Mitchill to Margaret Miller, 8 April 1806, Carolyn H. Sung, "Catharine Mitchill's Letters from Washington 1806–1812," *Quarterly Journal of the Library of Congress*, 34 (July 1977), 175.

29. John Quincy Adams, *Memoirs*, Vol. I, 268, 30 October 1803.

30. Ibid., Vol. I, 265, 23 October 1803.

31. Cutler and Cutler, *Life, Journal, and Correspondence*, Vol. II, . 116, 9 January, 1803.

32. Hung, *First Forty Years*, 14.

33. Hutson, *Religion*, 91.

34. Viator (Joseph Varnum), *The Washington Sketch Book* (New York, 1864), 107.

35. Hutson, *Religion*, 96.

36. Ibid., 93.

Chapter 3

1. This vignette is compiled from accounts in Virginia Van der Veer Hamilton, *Hugo Black: The Alabama Years* (Baton Rouge, LA: Louisiana State University Press, 1972); Steve Suitts, *Hugo Black of Alabama: How His Roots and Early Career Shaped the Great Champion of the Constitution* (Montgomery: NewSouth Books, 2005); and William H. Pryor Jr., Symposium on Law & Politics as Vocation, Address: *The Murder of Father James Coyle, The Prosecution of Edwin Stephenson, and the True Calling of Lawyers*, Vol. 20, Notre Dame Journal of Ethics and Public Policy, No. 401, 2006.

2. Dennis J. Hutchinson, Review, *Michigan Law Review of Hugo Black: A Biography*, by Roger K. Newman (New York: Pantheon, 1994) xiv, 741, (93 Mich. L. Rev. 1885), May 1995.

3. Ibid.

4. Ibid.

5. *Everson v. Board of Education of Ewing Tp.*, 330 U.S. 1 3 (1947).

6. Ibid., 3.

7. *Cochran v. Louisiana State Board of Education*, 281 U.S. 370 (1930).

8. 330 U.S. at 15.

9. Saul K. Padover, *The Complete Madison* (New York: Harper and Brothers, 1953), 301.

10. *Barron v. City of Council of Baltimore*, 32 U.S. 243, 247, 250 (1833).

11. US Constitution, Amendment XV, Section 1.

12. US Constitution, Amendment XIV, Section 1.

13. *Jaffree v. Board of School Commissioners*, 554 F. supp. 1104, 1126 (S.D. Ala. 1983).

14. *Lemon v. Kurtzmann*, 403 U.S. 602, 614 (1971).

15. Dallin Oakes; quoted by Joel F. Hansen, *Brigham Young University Law Review*, 1978, 647.

16. *Wallace v. Jaffree*, 472 US, 107 (internal citations omitted).

17. *Katcoff v. Marsh*, 755 F.2d 223 (2d. Cir. 1985).

18. *Commonwealth v. Chambers*; 599 A 2d 630, 643–644 (Pa. 1991).

19. *Olean Times Herald*, 6 April 1992, A–1, see also *State of Florida v. George T. Broxson*, Case no. 90-02930 CF (1st Jud. Cir. Ct., Walton County, Florida, 1992).

20. *Alexander v. Nacogdoches School District*, Civil Action 9:91CV144 (E.D. Tex. 1991).

Chapter 4

1. *Alexander v. Nacogdoches School District*, Civil Action 9:91CV144 (E.D. Tex. 1991).

2. Ibid., 2.

3. Ibid., 62.

4. Ibid., 120.

5. Ibid., 141.

6. Roger Baldwin, *Liberty Under the Soviets* (New York: Vanguard Press, 1928), 8–9.

7. Ibid., 10.

8. Ibid.

9. Ibid.

10. *Soviet Russia Today*, September 1934.

11. *Lamson*, 195.

12. *Investigation of Communist Propaganda*, House Report 2290, 17 January 1931, 56–57.

13. William A. Donohue, *The Politics of the American Civil Liberties Union* (New Brunswick: Transaction Books, 1985), 4.

14. *Lamson*, 188.

15. Jon Winokur, *The Portable Curmudgeon* (New York: New American Library, 1987), 170.

16. *Review of the News*, 13 August 1975.

17. *Constitution of the Union of Soviet Socialist Republics*, Article 124, 1947.

18. *Scopes v. State*, 289 S.W. 363 (Tenn. 1927).

19. Author interview with Rees Lloyd, 11 July 2006.

20. Thomas M. Landy, "What's Missing from This Picture," *Commonweal*, Vol. 119, Iss. 17, 9 October 1992 17.

21. *Newman v. Piggie Park Enterprises*, 390 U.S. 400 (1968).

22. *Alyeska Pipeline Co. v. Wilderness Society*, 421 U.S. 240 (1975).

23. Lloyd interview, 11 July 2006.

24. *McLean v. Arkansas Board of Education*, 723 F.2d. 45.

25. Ezra 7:24 (NIV).

26. John W. Whitehead, "Tax Exemption and Churches: A Historical and Constitutional Analysis," 22 *Cumberland Law Review* 521, 524 (1991–92).

27. R. E. McMaster, *Wealth for All* (Whitefish, : A. N., Inc., 1982), 85.

28. Robert A. Caro, *Master of the Senate: The Years of Lyndon Johnson* (New York: Alfred A. Knopf, 2002), 546.

29. James D. Davidson, *Why Churches Cannot Endorse or Oppose Political Candidates*, 40 Rev. of Religious Research 16 (1998); note 37, 21.

30. Letter from Lyndon Johnson to J. R. Parten, 3 June 1954, LBJ Library Dougherty, Dudley June 1954 File.

31. For a description of the historical background to the 1934 amendment see Wilfred R. Caron and Deirdre Dessingue, *IRC § 501(c)(3): Practical and Constitutional Implications of "Political" Activity Resolutions*, 2 J.L. & Pol. 169, 185–87 (1985).

32. 100 Cong. Rec. 9604 (1954).

33. Robert C. Albright, "Senate Votes Eisenhower Tax Revision Bill," *63 to 9*, Wash. Post & Times Herald, 3 July 1954, 1, col. 1.

34. *Branch Ministries, Inc. v. Rossotti*, 40 F. Supp. 2d.15, 17 (D.D.C. 1999).

35. Associated Press, 17 September 2006, "IRS Orders Church to Turn Over Papers."

36. Martin Luther King Jr., "Knock at Midnight," cited in *I Have a Dream: Writings and Speeches That Changed the World* (San Francisco: HarperCollins, 1992).

Chapter 5

1. Laurie Goodstein,"Churches on Right Seek Right to Back Candidates," *New York Times*, 3 February 2002.

2. Steve Miller, "Hillary Courts Blacks at Church Services," *Washington Times*, 6 November 2000, A1.

3. Dennis M. Mahoney, "Falwell Stumps for Bush at Church," *Columbus Dispatch*, 6 November 2000, 3C.

4. Sandra Sobieraj, "Gore Team Campaigns Through Midwest," AP, 6 November 2000.

5. Richard N. Ostling, "Some Clergy Deliver Political Words," Assoc. Press, 5 November 2000.

6. Ibid.

7. Office of the Press Secretary, "Remarks by the President to African American Religious and Community Leaders," M2 Presswire, 1 November 2000.

8. Derrick Z. Jackson, "Will Blacks Save Gore in Florida?," *Boston Globe*, 1 November 2000, A19.

9. Ana Mendieta, *Bush Endorsement Ripped*, *Chicago Sun-Times*, 1 November 2000, 34.

10. Sean Scully, "Democrats' Visits Could Cost Churches Tax-Exempt Status," *Washington Times*, 3 Nov., 2000, A11.

11. Sean Scully, "Cigarette Swap for Voting Skews Race, GOP Says," *Washington Times*, 7 November 2000, A7; *see also* James Jefferson, "Ark. Governor Criticizes Own State," AP, 6 November 2000 (quoting Arkansas Governor Mike Huckabee as saying, "They're lining up buses at minority churches, loading them up and hauling them to the polls as soon as church is over.").

12. Christopher Hitchens, "GI Jesus," Slate.com, October 2006. (www.slate.com/id/2150801/).

13. Ibid.

14. Ibid.

15. Robert Rutland, ed., *The Papers of James Madison*, Vol. VIII (Chicago: University of Chicago Press, 1973), 299, 304.

16. Richard B. Morris, ed., *The Encyclopedia of American History*, Bicentennial ed. (New York: Harper and Row, 1976), 820.

17. Robert L. Cord, *Separation of Church and State: Historical Fact and Current Fiction* (New York: Lambeth Press, 1982), 4.

18. Ibid.

19. Letter, October 2000, Barry Lynn, Americans United for Separation of Church and State.

20. Ibid.

21. Congressional Record: 8 July 2004 (House), H5385-H5386.

22. Author interview with John Hostetler, 18 July 2006.

23. S. 438, 96th Congress, 1st Session, 125 Congressional Record. 2863 (1979); S. 481, 97th Congress, 1st Session, 127 Congressional Record. S1284 (daily ed. 16 February 1981).

24. Jennifer Harper, "Majority in U.S. Believes in God," *Washington Times*, 25 December 2005.

BIBLIOGRAPHY

Ahlstrom, Sydney E. *A Religious History of the American People.* New Haven, CT: Yale University Press, 1972.

Antieau, Chester James, Arthur T. Downey, and Edward C. Roberts. *Freedom from Federal Establishment: Formation and History of the First Amendment Religion Clauses.* Milwaukee: Bruce, 1964.

Antieau, Chester James, Phillip Mark Carroll, and Thomas Carroll Burke. *Religion Under the State Constitutions.* Brooklyn, NY: Central Book Company, 1965.

Barton, David. *Original Intent: The Courts, The Constitution, & Religion.* Aledo: Wallbuilders Press, 1996.

Berger, Raoul. *Government by Judiciary: The Transformation of the Fourteenth Amendment.* Cambridge, MA: Harvard University Press, 1977.

Brant, Irving. *The Bill of Rights: Its Origin and Meaning.* Indianapolis, IN: The Bobbs-Merrill Company, 1965.

Briceland, Alan V. "Thomas Jefferson's Epitaph: Symbol of a Lifelong Crusade Against 'Those Who Would 'Usurp the Throne of God.'" 29 *Journal of Church and State* 285 (1987).

Bridenbaugh, Carl. *Mitre and Sceptre: Transatlantic Faiths, Ideas, Personalities & Politics, 1689–1775.* New York: Oxford University Press, 1962.

Boorstin, Daniel J. "The Founding Fathers and the Courage to Doubt," in *James Madison on Religious Liberty,* ed. Robert S. Alley. Buffalo, NY: Prometheus Books, 1985.

Borden, Morton. "Federalist, Antifederalist, and Religious Freedom." 21 *Journal of Church and State* 469 (1979).

Brownfield, Allen C. "The Constitutional Intent Concerning Matters of Church and State," 5 *William and Mary Law Review* 174 (1964).

_____. *James Madison.* 6 vols. Indianapolis, IN: The Bobbs-Merrill Company, 1941–61.

_____. *James Madison: The Father of the Constitution, 1787–1800.* Indianapolis, IN: The Bobbs-Merrill Company, 1950.

_____. "The Madison Heritage." 35 *New York University Law Review* 882 (1960).

_____. "Madison: On the Separation of Church and State." 8 *William and Mary Quarterly* 3 (3rd series, January 1951).

Butler, Paul M., and Alfred L. Scanlan. "Wall of Separation—Judicial Gloss on the First Amendment" *37 Notre Dame Lawyer* 288 (1962).

Cahn, Edmond. "The 'Establishment of Religion' Puzzle." 36 *New York University Law Review* 1274 (1961).

Church, Forrest. *The Separation of Church and State: Writings on a Fundamental Freedom by America's Founders.* Boston: Beacon Press, 2004.

Commager, Henry Steele. *The Empire of Reason: How Europe Imagined and America Realized the Enlightenment.* Garden City: Doubleday, 1977.

Cooley, Thomas. *A Treatise on the Constitutional Limitations.* 5th ed. Boston: Little, Brown, and Company, 1883.

_____. *The General Principles of Constitutional Law in the United States of America.* Boston: Little, Brown, and Company, 1880.

Cord, Robert L. "Church-State Separation: Restoring the 'No Preference' Doctrine of the First Amendment." 9 *Harvard Journal of Law and Public Policy* 129 (1986).

_____. "Neo-Incorporation: The Burger Court and the Due Process Clause of the Fourteenth Amendment." 44 *Fordham Law Review* 215 (1975).

_____. *Separation of Church and State: Historical Fact and Current Fiction.* New York: Lambeth Press, 1982.

_____. "Understanding the First Amendment." *National Review* 26 (22 January 1982).

Dreisbach, Daniel L. *Real Threat and Mere Shadow: Religious Liberty and the First Amendment.* Westchester: Crossway Books, 1987.

_____. *Thomas Jefferson and the Wall of Separation Between Church and State.* New York: New York University Press, 2002.

Drinan, Robert E. "The Novel 'Liberty' Created by the *McCollum* Decision." 39 *Georgetown Law Review* 216 (1951).

Donohue, William A. *The Politics of the American Civil Liberties Union.* New Brunswick: Transaction Books, 1985.

Eastland, Terry, ed. *Religious Liberty in the Supreme Court: The Cases That Define the Debate over Church and State.* Grand Rapids: William B. Eerdmans Publishing Company, 1993.

Eidsmoe, John. *The Christian Legal Advisor.* Milford: Mott Media, 1984.

Fleet, Elizabeth, ed. "Madison's 'Detached Memorandum.'" 3 *William and Mary Quarterly* 535 (3rd series, 1946).

Foote, Henry Wilder. *The Religion of Thomas Jefferson.* Boston: Beacon Press, 1947.

Gaustad, Edwin S. "A Disestablished Society: Origins of the First Amendment." 11 *Journal of Church and State* 409 (1969).

Gould, William D. "The Religious Opinions of Thomas Jefferson." 20 *Mississippi Valley Historical Review* 191 (1933).

Grant, George. *Trial and Error: The American Civil Liberties Union and Its Impact on Your Family.* Franklin: Adroit Press, 1989.

Hall, Thomas Cuming. *The Religious Background of American Culture.* Boston: Little, Brown, and Company, 1930.

Hamilton, Virginia Van der Veer. *Hugo Black: The Alabama Years.* Baton Rouge: Louisiana State University Press, 1972.

Hammett, Harold D. "The Homogenized Wall." 53 *American Bar Association Journal* 929 (1967).

Handy, Robert T. A. *Christian America: Protestant Hopes and Historical Realities.* New York: Oxford University Press, 1971.

Hentoff, Nat. "The Case of the Godless License Plate," *The Washington Post,* 8 November 1986, sec. A, 23.

Hitchcock, James. "The Supreme Court and Religion: Historical Overview and Future Prognosis." 24 *Saint Louis University Law Journal* 183 (1980).

Hitchens, Christopher. *Thomas Jefferson: Author of America.* New York: HarperCollins Publishers, 2005.

Hodge, A. A. "The Christian Foundation of American Politics." 5 *Journal of Christian Reconstruction* 36, no. 1 (Summer 1978).

Howe, Mark DeWolfe. *Cases on Church and State in the United States.* Cambridge, MA: Harvard University Press, 1952.

_____. *The Constitutional Question: Religion and the Free Society.* Fund for the Republic Pamphlet, 1958.

_____. *The Garden and the Wilderness: Religion* and *Government in American Constitutional History.* Chicago: University of Chicago Press, 1965.

Hofstadter, Richard. *The American Political Tradition.* London: Jonathan Cape, 1962.

_____. *The Paranoid Style in American Politics.* New York: Alfred A. Knopf, 1965.

Hudson, Winthrop S. *Religion in America: An Historical Account of the Development of American Religious Life.* New York: Charles Scribner's Sons, 1965.

Hutson, James H. *Religion and the Founding of the American Republic.* Washington: Library of Congress, 1998.

James, Charles Fenton. *Documentary History of the Struggle for Religious Liberty in Virginia.* Lynchburg, VA: J. P. Bell Company, 1900.

Jordan, W. K. *The Development of Religious Toleration in England,* Ill. Cambridge, MA: Harvard University Press, 1938.

Kauper, Paul G. "Church and State: Cooperative Separatism." 60 *Michigan Law Review* 1 (1961).

_____. *The Higher Law and the Rights of Man in a Revolutionary Society*. Washington DC: American Enterprise Institute for Public Policy Research, 1974.

_____. "Released Time and Religious Liberty: A Further Reply." 53 *Michigan Law Review* 233 (1954).

_____. *Religion and the Constitution*. Baton Rouge: Louisiana State University Press, 1964.

_____. "Separation of Church and State—A Constitutional View." 9 *Catholic Lawyer* 32 (1963).

Kik, J. Marcellus. *Church and State: The Story of Two Kingdoms*. New York: Thomas Nelson and Sons, 1963.

Klenk, John. "President Reagan's Proposed Voluntary School Prayer Amendment." *Backgrounder*. Washington DC: Republican Study Committee, 1982.

Levy, Leonard W. *Constitutional Opinions: Aspects of the Bill of Rights*. New York: Oxford University Press, 1986.

Lipscomb, Andrew A., and Albert Ellery Bergh. *The Writings of Thomas Jefferson*. 20 vols. Washington DC: The Thomas Jefferson Memorial Association, 1905.

McCarthy, Mary Barbara. "The Application of the First Amendment to the States by the Fourteenth Amendment of the Constitution." 22 *Notre Dame Lawyer* 400 (1947).

Madison, James. *Writings*. New York: Library of America, 1999.

McDonald, Forrest. *Novus Ordo Seclorum: The Intellectual Origins of the Constitution*. Lawrence: University Press of Kansas, 1985.

Meacham, Jon. *American Gospel: God, the Founding Fathers, and the Making of a Nation*. New York: Random House, 2006.

Mead, Sidney E. *The Lively Experiment: The Shaping of Christianity in America*. New York: Harper and Row, 1963.

_____. "Neither Church nor State: Reflections on James Madison's 'Line of Separation.'" 10 *Journal of Church and State* 349 (1968).

_____. "Religion, Constitutional Federalism, Rights, and the Court." 14 *Journal of Church and State* 191 (1972).

_____. "Thomas Jefferson's 'Fair Experiment'—Religious Freedom." 23 *Religion in Life* 566 (1953–54).

Meese, Edwin, III. "Toward a Jurisprudence of Original Intention." II, no. 1 *Benchmark* 1 (January–February 1986).

Miller, Perry. "The Contribution of the Protestant Churches to Religious Liberty in Colonial America." 4 *Church History* 57 (1935).

Niebuhr, H. Richard. *The Kingdom of God in America.* New York: Harper and Row, 1937.

Padover, Saul K., ed. *The Washington Papers.* New York: Harper and Brothers, 1955.

_____, ed. *The Complete Jefferson.* New York: Tudor Publishing Co., 1943.

Parsons, Wilfrid. *The First Freedom: Considerations on Church and State in the United States.* New York: Declan X. McMullen, 1948.

Pfeffer, Leo. "Church and State: Something Less Than Separation." 19 *University of Chicago Law Review* 1 (1951).

_____. *Church, State and Freedom.* Boston: Beacon Press, 1953; revised edition, 1967.

_____. *Creeds in Competition: A Creative Force in American Culture.* New York: Harper and Row, 1958.

_____. "The Deity in American Constitutional History." 23 *Journal of Church and State* 215 (1981).

_____. *God, Caesar, and the Constitution: The Court as Referee of Church-State Confrontation.* Boston, MA: Beacon Press, 1975.

_____. *The Liberties of an American: The Supreme Court Speaks.* Boston: Beacon Press, 1956.

_____. "Released Time and Religious Liberty: A Reply." 53 *Michigan Law Review* 91

_____. "Religion-Blind Government." 15 *Stanford Law Review* 389 (1963).

_____. *Religious Freedom*. Skokie, IL: National Textbook Company; American Civil Liberties Union, 1977.

_____. "Uneasy Trinity: Church, State, and Constitution." 2 *Civil Liberties Review* 138 (1975).

Randall, Henry S. *The Life of Thomas Jefferson*. 3 vols. New York: Derby and Jackson, 1858.

Rehnquist, William H. "The Notion of a Living Constitution." 54 *Texas Law Review* 693 (1976).

Rice, Charles E. "Congress and the Supreme Court's Jurisdiction." 27 *Villanova Law Review* 959 (1981–82).

_____. "Conscientious Objection to Public Education: The Grievance and the Remedies." 1978 *Brigham Young University Law Review* 847 (1978).

_____. "Constitutional Checks Upon the Judiciary." Speech on Judicial Power in the United States, American Enterprise Institute for Public Policy Research, Washington. DC, 1–2 October 1981.

_____. "Lawlessness." 2, no. 2 *Journal of Christian Reconstruction* 22 (Winter 1975).

Rossiter, Clinton. *The Political Thought of the American Revolution*. New York: Harcourt, Brace and World, 1963.

_____. *Seedtime of the Republic: The Origin of the American Tradition of Political Liberty*. New York: Harcourt, Brace and World, 1953.

_____. *Liberty*. New York: Harcourt, Brace and World, 1953.

_____. "Which Jefferson Do You Quote?" 13 *The Reporter* 33 (1955).

Rushdoony, Rousas John. *Christianity and the State*. Vallecito, CA: Ross House Books, 1986.

_____. "The Freedom of the Church." no. 16 *Chalcedon Position Paper* (1980).

_____. "The Myth of an American Enlightenment." 3, no. 1 *Journal of Christian Reconstruction* 69 (Summer 1976).

_____. *The Nature of the American System.* Fairfax, VA: Thoburn Press, 1965.

_____. *Politics of Guilt and Pity.* Fairfax, VA: Thoburn Press, 1978.

_____. "Religion and the State," no. 152 *The Chalcedon Report* (April 1978).

_____. "Religious Liberty," No. 12 *Chalcedon Position Paper.*

_____. "The State as an Establishment of Religion," in *Freedom and Education: Pierce v. Society of Sisters Reconsidered,* eds. Donald P. Kommers and Michael J. Wahoske. Notre Dame, IN: University of Notre Dame Law School, 1978.

_____. *This Independent Republic.* Fairfax, VA: Thoburn Press, 1964.

Rutland, Robert Allen. *The Birth of the Bill of Rights, 1776–1791.* Chapel Hill, NC: University of North Carolina Press, 1955.

_____. "James Madison's Dream: A Secular Republic," in *James Madison on Religious Liberty,* ed. Robert S. Alley. Buffalo, NY: Prometheus Books, 198.

_____. ed. *The Papers of George Mason.* 3 vols. Chapel Hill, NC: University of North Carolina Press, 1970.

Singer, C. Gregg. *A Theological Interpretation of American History* Philadelphia, PA: Presbyterian and Reformed, 1964.

Story, Joseph. "Christianity a Part of the Common Law." IX *American Jurist and Law Magazine* 346 (April 1833).

_____. *Commentaries on the Constitution of the United States.* 3rd edition, 2 vols. Boston, MA: Little, Brown, and Company, 1858.

Suitts, Steve. *Hugo Black of Alabama: How His Roots and Early Career Shaped the Great Champion of the Constitution.* Montgomery: NewSouth Books, 2005.

Sweet, William Warren. *Religion in Colonial America.* New York: Charles Scribner's Sons, 1942.

"Symposium: Religion and the State." 14 *Law and Contemporary Problems* 1 (1949).

Tuveson, Ernest L. *Redeemer Nation: The Idea of America's Millennial Role.* Chicago: University of Chicago Press, 1968.

Wood, James E. Jr., ed. *Religion and the State: Essays in Honor of Leo Pfeffer.* Waco, TX: Baylor University Press, 1985.

INDEX

ABOUT THE AUTHOR

Stephen Mansfield is the *New York Times* bestselling author of *The Faith of George W. Bush, The Faith of the American Soldier, Benedict XVI: His Life and Mission,* and *Never Give In: The Extraordinary Character of Winston Churchill,* among other works of history, biography, and contemporary culture. His interest in First Amendment religion issues arises from his decades of work among American churches and his efforts on behalf of religious liberty in the Middle East. Stephen lives in downtown Nashville, Tennessee, with his wife, Beverly, who is also an author as well as a songwriter and producer. For more information, log on to www.mansfieldgroup.com.

ACKNOWLEDGMENTS

Though it is by the grace of God that the author of this book is a historian and not a lawyer, the thoughts of some of America's finest legal minds do grace these pages.

Harvard professor Alan Dershowitz was typically brilliant and unsparing in my interview with him, and I am grateful both for the gift of his time as well as the gift of his intellectual passion. Barry Lynn, leading light of Americans United for the Separation of Church and State, was again, as I have always found him to be, knowledgeable, patient, and kind. Judge Andrew Napolitano was typically hilarious, uncommonly wise, and unapologetically Italian. It is not hard to understand why he is beloved nationwide. Rees Lloyd, formerly of the ACLU and currently of the American Legion, moved me with his devotion to the memory of Cesar Chavez as well as with his devotion to justice. My time with him was an honor.

Scholars, thinkers, and activists from a wide variety of disciplines also graced me with their wisdom. John Seigenthaler Sr., a dean of American journalism, helped me understand the role of the First Amendment in recent American history, and David Hudson of the First Amendment Center at Vanderbilt University helped me understand the role of religion in recent American law. Mark Beliles of the Providence Foundation and David Barton of Wallbuilders, friends and mentors, spoke to me both about the original intent of the founding generation and the current status of Establishment Clause legislation. Michael Newdow took time from his busy work in an emergency room to explain the thinking that has placed him at the forefront of national attention, and Congressman Walter Jones, Congressman Ron Paul, and

Congressman John Hostetler each carved out time from their obviously busy schedules to help me understand their legislative battles.

My work on this book was made a joy in large part because my own "Dream Team" of lawyers was comprised of some of my dearest friends. David Toberty and Kevin Ikenberry have taught me both a love of learning and a love of the law through the years. They have made my life rich. Jim Foster offered such wise guidance that I was painfully reminded that I once tried to talk him out of going to law school. And Steve Voigt, great legal mind and fire-breathing activist, showed me why he is one of the rising young lawyers in Philadelphia.

Once again the guiding hand of my elder brother, George Grant, is evident in my writing, and this time he is joined by Emily Mulloy Prather, whose research genius, it is not going too far to say, transformed this book. As always, I am grateful to Beverly Darnall and her amazing team at Chartwell Literary Group. No author or publisher should be without their skills, and I am grateful beyond words that I have not had to be.

The expertise and wisdom of my own team has freed me not only to write but to dream. Esther Fedorkevich is both agent and friend, Susan Levine gets me where I need to be when I need to be there, and Ruth Chodniewicz gets my message where it has not gone before. On this project, Todd Bulgarino of TechOptions helped me recover from a computer crash and did it with such grace and humor that he kept me from a personal crash as well. To all, I am beyond grateful.

Finally, when an author like me paints his meaning in the broad strokes that a book like this demands, each color and hue he uses has been provided by some far more devoted scholar, some far greater yet usually unknown mind. I am not unaware that I am summarizing here in a few pages the scholarship of men and women who have devoted lifetimes to this theme. Thank God, then, for the scholar, whose desk is an altar and whose learning is a gift to the ages.